NEW GRANGE

and other incised tumuli in Ireland

GEORGE COFFEY

Dolphin Archaeologies

Prehistoric Rock Art of Argyll by Ronald W. B. Morris

Mesolithic Cultures of Britain by S. Palmer

The Megalithic Art of the Maltese Islands by Michael Ridley

GEORGE COFFEY

NEW GRANGE

and other incised tumuli in Ireland

DOLPHIN
PRESS

Published in Great Britain by
The Dolphin Press, Link House, West Street, Poole, Dorset.

First published 1912

ISBN 0 85642 041 7

This Edition Copyright (C) 1977 Blandford Press

Dolphin Studio Production

Printed and Bound in Great Britain by
Butler and Tanner
Frome, Somerset.

CONTENTS

FOREWORD

The great prehistoric chambered tomb of New Grange lies in the bend of the Boyne, north of Dublin and west of Drogheda. It is one of a group of prehistoric tombs forming one of the great cemeteries of ancient Europe. Until the end of the seventeenth century it was a huge grass-covered mound and then the chamber tomb was found. Edward Lhwyd, Keeper of the Ashmolean Museum at Oxford, was travelling in Ireland at the time and wrote in a letter dated 15 December 1699, 'The most remarkable curiosity we saw by the way was a stately Mount at a place called New Grange near Drogheda; having a number of huge stones pitch'd on end round about it, and a single one on the top. The gentleman of the village (one Mr. Charles Campbell) observing that under the green turf this mount was wholly composed of stones, and having occasion for some, employ'd his servants to carry off a considerable parcel of them; till they came at last to a very broad flat stone, rudely carved, and placed edgewise at the bottom of the mount. This they discovered to be the door of a cave, which had a long entry leading to it.' Thus was discovered one of the finest megalithic monuments in the world, and one of the earliest and most remarkable examples of early architecture in western Europe.

The last two and a half centuries have seen much speculation about the name and nature of the New Grange chambered mound. Edward Lhwyd himself, percipient and brilliant antiquary that he was, thought the site was pre-Roman: 'some place of sacrifice or burial of the ancient Irish' he wrote. Others thought it Danish, or Phoenician, or Egyptian or Druidic. Sir Richard Colt Hoare, who travelled in Ireland in the early nineteenth century, was inclined to 'attribute this singular temple to some of the Celtic or Belgic tribes who poured in upon us from the continent of Gaul.'

The first person to describe New Grange objectively and to study it in its widest European contexts was George Coffey (1857 - 1916). A student at Trinity College, Dublin, intended to be a lawyer, his antiquarian interests prevailed: in 1897 he became Curator of Irish Antiquities in the National Museum of Ireland and the first Keeper: he was also Professor of Archaeology in the Royal Hibernian Academy. A man of wide interests and great learning, he was described in his obituary in the *Journal of the Royal Society of Antiquaries of Ireland*, as a noteable figure with 'striking presence, flexible intelligence, fine mental quality, and power of lucid and eloquent exposition'. Coffey wrote papers on New Grange in the *Transactions* and *Proceedings* of the Royal

Irish Academy and in the *Journal of the Royal Society of Antiquaries of Ireland*, and in 1912 put these papers in a revised form into his book which is now reprinted after sixty years.

When Coffey first studied New Grange in 1890, as he tells us 'it was a generally accepted view that the spirals there were the immediate precursors of the spirals of Early Christian times and I therefore attributed much too late a date for them'. He then said, 'In more recent studies I abandoned this view and adopted a much earlier date'; and the sub-title of his book in 1912 was 'The influence of Crete and the Aegean in the extreme west of Europe in early times.' He approved of the comparison made between New Grange and the Treasury of Atreus at Mycenae and while he appreciated the comparisons made between the spirals at New Grange and those of Minoan Crete, he was not prepared to accept the view of the great French archaeologist Joseph Dechelette that New Grange was linked with the pre-Mycenean world. He came down firmly on the side of Mycenean comparisons and from Coffey's time onwards New Grange has been vaguely referred to as a Bronze Age monument.

In the mid-fifties the late Professor Sean O'Riordain asked me to co-operate with him in writing a sort of sequel to Coffey: he died in 1957 when the book was little more than half done. It was eventually published in 1964 under the title of *New Grange and the Bend of the Boyne*. In that book we were able to publish a great number of new photographs taken by O'Riordain himself, and his pupils and friends. We discussed the date at length and said 'we suggest that it might have been built at 2500 B.C. ± 250 years' and added, 'we realise this is much earlier than both of us have argued on several occasions before, when a date between 1900 and 1600 B.C. seemed probable'.

In the summer of 1962 Professor M. J. O'Kelly, a pupil of O'Riordain's who succeeded him in the chair of archaeology at Cork, began excavations at New Grange which have continued annually until the present moment. His work has revolutionised our knowledge of the monument and, when fully published, will provide the answers to the questions being asked from the time of Edward Lhwyd onwards. He has made us think of the monument not merely as a great tomb but as a place of ritual significance - as a kind of temple. He has also been able to provide exact dates by radiocarbon analysis and says that they 'may be put together to give a round figure date of 2500 B.C.' (*Antiquity*, 1969, 141; see also *Antiquity*, 1972, 226). But this is an uncalibrated date based on radiocarbon years: the calendar date for New Grange must now be nearer 3000 B.C. than 2500 B.C.

New Grange is then back to the horizon of Minoan Crete as Dechelette suggested, but nowadays we do not see it as an outpost of Aegean civilisation, as Coffey, very tentatively thought it might be. We now think that the influence of the east Mediterranean on north-western Europe in Prehistoric times is very little and that the megalithic monuments may well be the product of local barbarian societies. New Grange in Ireland, and Gavrinis in Brittany, now seem to many present-day archaeologists as triumphs of local inspiration and architecture. If this is so, it is even more than ever necessary to have Coffey's sober and careful account of the Boyne tombs available to us while we re-assess the place of megalithic monuments in the most ancient history of western Europe.

Glyn Daniel

Disney Professor of Archaeology
University of Cambridge

SCALE.

0   ¼   ½   ¾   1 Mile.

CLOGHALEA

Fort

DOWTH HO.

Fort

J

Fort

Tumulus

Castle

Church

St. Bernard's Well

F

Tumuli

F G H

Tumulus

E

Stones

Standing Stone

Standing Stone

D

C

Tumulus

B

Tumulus

A

Tumulus

Fort

KNOWTH HO.

Tumulus

Fort

NEW GRANGE HO.

BROE HO.

ROSSNAREE HO.

RIVER BOYNE

Ford.

Ford

Ford

NEW GRANGE

Five miles west of Drogheda, and thence extending about three miles along the northern bank of the Boyne towards Slane, are the remains of the most remarkable of the pre-Christian cemeteries of Ireland. The accompanying map, reduced from the six-inch Ordnance Survey, shows the positions of the existing sepulchral mounds, standing stones, and raths within the group. The cemetery has been identified as the *Brugh na Boinne* of the manuscripts, more particularly described in the *Senchas na Relec*, or History of the Cemeteries, preserved in the Leabhar na hUidhri, and in the *Dindsenchus* of the Book of Ballymote.

Of the three principal mounds, at Dowth, New Grange, and Knowth, situated about a mile apart, and in sight one from the other, that at New Grange is the largest and best known, and will be described first. The chamber of this tumulus has been open since about the year 1699, when it was visited and described by the Welsh antiquary, Edward Lhwyd. Since then it has attracted the attention of many archaeologists on the Continent as well as in these islands.

Fig 1. Tumulus at New Grange, from a photo taken in 1891

As seen from the road the appearance of the mound is rather disappointing. It is overgrown with trees and bushes which obscure its outline, and lend to it the character of one of the many wooded knolls of the surrounding country. Moreover, the rising ground on which it stands foreshortens it and takes from its apparent bulk. Indeed, the great size of the monument cannot be realized until the visitor has walked round it.

A few yards outside the base, the tumulus appears to have been originally surrounded by a circle of standing stones, twelve of which may still be traced (see Plan, fig. 2). Four of these stones, forming portion of the circle near the entrance, are of great size, measuring, respectively, in height 7 feet, 6 feet 8 in., 8 feet, and 6 feet above the ground, and in girth 18, 20, 19 and 15 feet. These four stones are shown in fig. 1. The rest are smaller, in some cases but a foot or two above the ground, with the exception of one on the east side, which appears to have fallen down, and is now level with the surface—it measures 11 feet in length. The interval between the three stones at the entrance, where the circle appears

New Grange before excavation

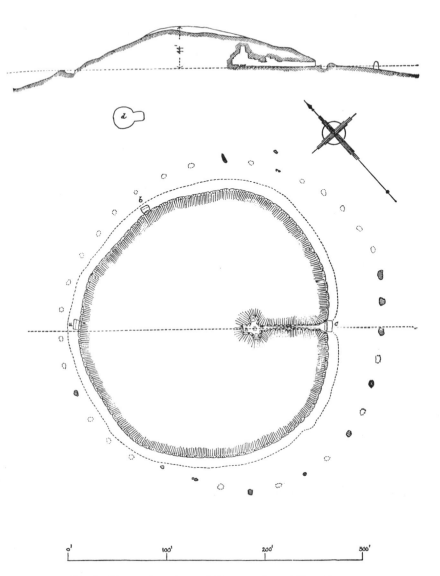

Fig 2. Plan and section of the tumulus at New Grange

unbroken, measures 30 feet from centre to centre, and will be
found to go nearly exactly into the distances between the other
stones, giving about thirty-five stones to the circle. It is possible
that the circle was never completed; but the regular manner in
which the existing stones are placed would indicate that they have
not been set up at random, but form portions of a circle which
originally consisted of, or was laid down for, thirty-five stones.

Aerial photograph of New Grange showing the recent excavations by Prof. M O'Kelly

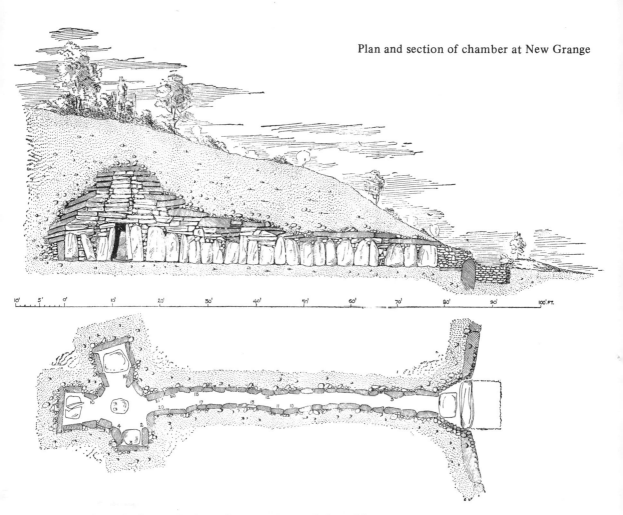

Plan and section of chamber at New Grange

Inside this circle a ditch and rampart, mainly of loose stones, runs round the base of the mound. It is difficult to say whether or not it is part of the original structure. For the greater part of the circumference it is well defined, but less so at the east side, for a portion of which it may be said to cease.

The mound or tumulus itself consists of an enormous cairn of loose stones, heaped within a curb of great stones, 8 to 10 feet long, laid on edge, and touching end to end, over which a thin covering of grass has grown. A similar arrangement is found at Dowth, and in the cairns of the Loughcrew Hills. In plan the tumulus is circular, and covers an area of about one acre, or, taking the circle of the standing stones, nearly two acres. The greatest diameter of the mound measures 280 feet. Its present height is 44 feet (see the Plan and Section). On the plan is a curiously constructed cell, marked *d*, apparently of Christian origin, possibly a hermit's, but concerning which nothing is known. The somewhat flattened top, also found at Knowth, is not an unusual feature in such structures. A retaining wall, or revetement of dry rubble, some five to six feet high, is built immediately on the base stones. This retaining wall, I have been informed, is a modern feature, and was made in the time of Mr. Tiernan, a former tenant of New Grange.

The entrance, it will be noticed, is clearly marked by the curving inwards of the curb-stones (see Plan). The same feature is strongly marked in the larger cairns on the Loughcrew Hills. We usually think of the entrance of a tumulus as concealed when the chamber was covered in. It is evident, from the manner in which it is marked by the curving inwards of the curb-stones, that this was not so in the case of passage-tombs such as at Loughcrew and New Grange. It is probable that the more prominent tombs were set apart for particular families or persons. The tumuli we are speaking of, it must not be forgotten, are grouped in cemeteries, and imply a more or less settled state of society; they appear to have been respected till the coming of the Danes, who, moreover, seem to have found no difficulty in finding the entrances through which they have generally been plundered. The supposition that the passage at New Grange was originally longer, is therefore, incorrect; as also the sections which show the mound produced to a dotted line ending at a standing stone symmetrically with the back slope. The large stone in front of the entrance is, in fact, one of the boundary stones, and marks the limit of the mound at that side. This stone, richly carved in spirals and lozenges, has been frequently described. Until recently its lower half was covered by the ground. But, in the year 1890, the monument having been lately scheduled under the Protection of Ancient Monuments Act of 1882, the earth was excavated in front, under the direction of the late Sir Thomas Deane, so as to expose the entire of its carved surface. Sir Thomas Deane's investigation brought to light two additional richly carved stones in the boundary circuit, and it is

Opposite: The interior of New Grange looking towards the passage from the main chamber

probable that further examination will add to the number. The two stones referred to are marked *a* and *b* on Plan (fig. 2), and will be more particularly described later. Pits have been sunk before them so as to expose the carving in a similar manner to the entrance stone. The sides of the mound, where it had ravelled out at the entrance, were, at the same time, trimmed and faced with dry walling. This takes somewhat from the sentiment of the monument, but may have been necessary for its protection.

Having sufficiently described the general appearance of the tumulus, we may enter its sepulchral chamber. Immediately in front of the entrance, and between it and the carved boundary stone already mentioned, lies a large flat stone, forming a sort of sill to the opening of the passage (see Plan, Plate I). This stone probably sealed the entrance, with the dimensions of which it roughly agrees. In a section of the chamber, drawn by Du Noyer, and published in Wilkinson's "Practical Geology and Ancient Architecture of Ireland," 1845, this stone is shown in an inclined position, as if it had been forced back from the entrance. And in the text Wilkinson says, "A large flat stone appears, from the peculiarity of its position, to have closed the entrance." A few feet above the opening, a horizontal slab, carved on its projecting face, should be noticed. It gives somewhat of an architectural character to the entrance, and is remarkable on that account as well as for its carving.

In general plan the passage and chamber are irregularly cruciform. The former measures 62 feet in length, and is formed of large stones, set on end, some 5 to 8 feet in height, roofed with flag-stones of great size. That at the entrance is 11 feet long, and the stone next but one somewhat longer. The average width of the passage is about 3 feet, but some 14 feet in from the entrance, the side stones meet at the top, rendering it necessary to creep on hands and knees for a distance of about six feet. After this point the passage presents no further difficulty. At the entrance it is 4 feet 9 in. high; it then rises gradually to about 6 feet through a distance of 26 feet. The headway is then reduced by the roofing-stone at that point, after which it rises rapidly by overlapping stones to 7 feet 10 in. at 43 feet from the entrance, when it suddenly falls again to 4 feet 10 in. The construction will be readily understood by reference to the section. After passing this point the passage rises rapidly by overlapping stones till merged in the roof of the chamber. The latter consists of a conical or funnel-shaped dome, formed of large flat stones laid horizontally and corbelled, or projecting inwards, one over the other, till closed by a single stone. In plan it is an irregular hexagon, and shows considerable enterprise in the fitting of the passage-roofing, and recesses. The principal dimensions of the chamber are—height, 19 feet 6 in.; end of passage to back of north recess, 18 feet; back of east to back of west recess, 21 feet. Something of an architectural character is given to the construction of this chamber by the carrying round its walls of the upright course of stone which lines the passage, and in places supports its roof. In the chamber, these

Plate II Corbelled roof of the chamber looking upwards

stones do not actually support the roof as at Dowth; the construction of the dome is practically independent of such support, and is incorrectly described by Sir W. Wilde as springing from this course of upright stones. The carvings for which the tumulus is noted are cut chiefly on these stones. The three recesses which give the plan its cruciform appearance are of unequal dimensions.

That on the east side is 8 feet 8 in. in depth; the north recess, 7 ft. 6 in.; and the west recess but 3 ft. 4 in. On the floor of each recess is placed a large stone basin or rude sarcophagus. The hollowed-out form of the basin is most marked in that in the east recess; that in the north recess is, unfortunately, broken—it shows but slight traces of having been hollowed, and might be described as a flat stone; it, however, no doubt served a similar purpose to those in the other recesses. A much more carefully wrought basin at present stands in the centre of the chamber. It was found in the east recess, and stood within the basin still in that recess. It has been recently moved into the centre, on the supposition that it originally occupied that position; but there seems to be no foundation for Wilkinson's statement that it originally stood in the centre, and, as I shall presently show, the evidence as to position establishes the contrary. This basin is remarkable for two cup depressions within the hollowed portion of the stone.

Previous Notices.—The reader is now sufficiently acquainted with the general features of the tumulus to follow with interest some of the previous notices of the monument. The tumulus has suffered much from dilapidation, and as the earlier descriptions differ on some points of detail, it is desirable to recover, as far as possible, from a comparison of these accounts, the state of the chamber when first entered in modern times. The earliest description of New Grange is contained in a letter of the Welsh antiquary, Edward Lhwyd, keeper of the Ashmolean Museum at Oxford. It is addressed to Dr. Tancred Robinson, of the Royal Society, and dated "Rathgate, near Linlithgow, Scotland, December 15, 1699. Doubt is expressed by Sir W. Wilde as to when the entrance was first discovered in modern times; the present letter sets that question at rest. I extract the passage in full:—

Transactions of the Royal Society, vol. xxvii., p. 603. Abridged Series, vol. v., p. 694.

"We continued not above three Days at Dublin, when we steer'd our Course towards the *Giant's Causeway*. The most remarkable Curiosity we saw by the way was a stately Mount at a place called *New Grange*, near *Drogheda*; having a number of huge Stones pitch'd on end round about it, and a single one on the Top. The Gentleman of the Village (one *Mr. Charles Campbel*) observing that under the green Turf this Mount was wholly composed of Stones, and having occasion for some, employ'd his Servants to carry off a considerable Parcel of them; till they came at last to a broad flat Stone, rudely Carved, and placed edgewise at the Bottom of the Mount. This they discover'd to be the Door of a Cave, which had a long Entry leading into it. At the first entering we were forced to creep; but still as we went on the Pillars on each side of us were higher and higher; and coming into the Cave we found it about 20 Foot high. In this Cave, on each hand of us, was a Cell or Apartment, and another went on straight forward opposite to the Entry. In those on each hand was a very broad shallow Bason of Stone, situated at the Edge. The Bason in the Right-Hand Apartment stood in another; that on the Left hand was single; and in the Apartment straight forward there was none at all. We observed that Water dropped into the right-hand Bason, tho' it had rained but little in many Days; and suspected that the lower Bason was intended to preserve the superfluous Liquor of the upper (whether this Water were Sacred, or whether it was for Blood in Sacrifice), that none might come to the Ground. The great Pillars round this cave, supporting the Mount, were not at all hewn or wrought; but were such rude Stones as those of *Abury* in *Wiltshire*, and rather more rude than those of *Stonehenge*. But those about the Basons, and some elsewhere, had such Barbarous Sculpture (*viz*. Spiral like a Snake, but without distinction of Head and Tail), as the fore-mentioned Stone at the entry of the Cave. There was no Flagging nor Floor to this Entry nor Cave; but any sort of loose Stones everywhere under Feet. They found several Bones in the Cave, and part of a Stag's (or else Elk's) Head, and some other things which I omit, because the Labourers differ'd in their Account of them. A Gold Coin of the Emperor *Valentinian*, being found near the Top of this Mount might bespeak it *Roman*; but that the rude Carving at the Entry and in the Cave seems to denote it a Barbarous Monument. So, the Coin proving it ancienter than any Invasion of the *Ostmans* or *Danes*; and the Carving and rude Sculpture, Barbarous; it should follow, that it was some Place of Sacrifice or Burial of the ancient *Irish*."

In a letter written some three months later, addressed to Rowlands, and dated Sligo, March 12, 1700, p. 336 and published in the latter's "Mona Antiqua Restaurata," Dublin, 1723, Lhwyd, who appears to have returned to Ireland in the meantime, repeats the description in nearly the same words. The particulars given are not, however, quite so full as in the former letter; it is, therefore, unnecessary to quote it at length. The stone on the top of the mound is mentioned in these words:—The "Mound or Barrow" is "of very considerable height, encompass'd with vast Stones pitch'd on End round the bottom of it; and having another lesser standing on the top." The state of the floor of the chamber is thus described:—"Under feet there were nothing but loose Stones of every size in Confusion; and amongst them a great many Bones of Beasts and some Pieces of Deers' Horns." These passages are worth quoting as tending to make more definite the statements of the previous letter as to the stone on top and state of the chamber. Sir W. Wilde does not appear to have looked up Lhwyd's first letter in the Transactions of the Royal Society, and so fell into the error of describing the extract from the letter, published in "A Collection of such Papers as were communicated to the Royal Society referring to some Curiosities in Ireland," Dublin 1726; also in the Abridged Series of the Philosophical Transactions vol. v. (in both cases without date), as a paraphrase of "Mr. Lhwyd's Essay," published in the "Mona Antiqua." It is really three months earlier; moreover, the second letter omits all mention of the discovery of the entrance by Mr. Campbel, also the important statement concerning things said to be found in the cave, but as to which the labourers differed, which fixes the date of the discovery of the entrance as shortly before Lhwyd's visit.

The next account of New Grange is found in Molyneux's "Discourse concerning Danish Mounds, Forts, and Towers in Ireland," published in 1725. It is accompanied by a plan of the chamber. Molyneux had visited the tumulus, and speaks from his own observation; his estimate of the height of the mound is, however, strangely astray. He states it is a thousand feet in circumference at the bottom; the flat surface at the top 300 feet; and that it rises the perpendicular about 150 feet. It is not necessary to quote Molyneux's general description of the entrance and chamber, but some of his statements deserve attention:—"The bottom of the cave and entry," he states, "is a rude sort of pavement, made of the same stones of which the mount is composed, not beaten or joined together, but loosely cast on the ground only to cover it. Along the middle of the cave, a slender quarry-stone, five or six feet long, lies on the floor, shaped like a pyramid, that once, as I imagine, stood upright, perhaps a central stone to those placed round the outside of the mount; but now 'tis fallen down. . . .When first the cave was opened, the bones of two dead bodies entire, not burnt, were found upon the floor, in likelihood the reliques of a husband and his wife, whose conjugal affection had joyn'd them in their grave. . . .

"In each of the three cells was placed upon the ground, a broad and shallow cistern, somewhat round, but rudely formed out of a kind of free-stone; they all were rounded a little at the bottom so as to be convex, and at the top were slightly hollowed, but their cavities contained but little; some of their brims or edges were sinuated or scolopt; the diameter of these cisterns was more than two foot wide, and in their height they measured about eighteen inches from the floor.

"The cell that lay upon the right hand was larger;. . . .the cistern it contained was better shaped, and in the middle of it was placed another smaller cistern, better wrought, and of a more curious make."

Molyneux also informs us that "about ten or twelve years since" two Roman gold coins, one of Valentinian, and the other of Theodosius, were found in removing some stones on the outside of the mound. The plan which accompanies Molyneux's account, which, he tells us, "Mr. Samuel Molyneux, a young gentleman of the College of Dublin, delineated with care and accuracy, upon the place, last summer," appears to be drawn with care. The general proportions of the chamber and passage are correctly shown, and the stones have been counted, though no dimensions are given. The basins in the three recesses are shown, and the stone alleged to have been seen lying in the centre of the chamber is shown on the plan in that position. A rude drawing of the eastern recess is also given, as well as drawings of the two Roman coins stated to be taken from the coins themselves.

In 1770, Governor Pownall, who had lately visited the locality, read a Paper before the Society of Antiquaries on the "Sepulchral Monument at New Grange" (printed in "Archaeologia," vol. ii). The Paper is of considerable length, and is illustrated by a sketch of the mound. No trees appear to have obscured its outline at that time, which is shown as that of a truncated cone, with flat top, rising above the trees of the surrounding fields. Pownall describes its appearance thus:—"The lanes about it are planted with rows of trees. And the country forms an ornamental landscape, uncommon in Ireland. The pyramid, if I may so call it, built on rising ground, and heaving its bulky mass over the tops of the trees and above the face of the country, with dimensions of a scale greater than the objects which surround it, appears, though now but a ruinous frustrum of what it once was, a superb and eminently magnificent monument." Pownall employed a Mr. Samuel Bouie, a local surveyor, to measure the mound and chamber; and the Paper is illustrated by plans and sections prepared from Bouie's measurements.

Bouie makes the height of the tumulus 42 feet. Pownall is inclined to estimate it at 56 feet from the horizontal line of the floor of the cave; and, adding the curve of the ground, he makes the altitude of the whole to be about 70 feet. The other dimensions agree nearly with Molyneux. Bouie's estimate of the height, it will be noticed, agrees nearly with the present section.

Pownall's description has been the chief source from which subsequent writers, including Petrie, Wilde, and Fergusson, in his "Rude Stone Monuments," have taken the dimensions and other particulars of New Grange. The sections and plans, though giving some general idea of the chamber, cannot be relied on in detail, and as regards the mound, as Fergusson says, "it is almost impossible to make out its form and dimensions from the plates published." Pownall makes no mention of the stone which Lhwyd says stood on the top of the mound. "The pyramid," he adds, "in its present state" is "but a ruin of what it was. It has long served as a stone-quarry to the country round about. All the roads in the neighbourhood are paved with its stones; immense quantities have been taken away." The following particulars are of interest:—The "Northern Tabernacle" of the chamber is described as having for its floor a large flat stone; the two side niches had no other floor but the natural ground, but had each of them a rock basin placed within them—that on the left side on the ground, and that on the right "upon a kind of base." The greater part of Pownall's Paper is taken up with historical conjectures and a lengthy investigation into which we need not follow him, of certain marks which he took to be traces of letters, and finally persuaded himself to be Phoenician numerals.

Pownall's plans and sections are reproduced by Ledwich in his "Antiquities of Ireland," published in 1803. New Grange is also described in Sir R. C. Hoare's "Tour in Ireland," 1806. He appears to have been the first to have noticed the two cup depressions within the basin in the east recess. Petrie wrote a short account of the monument in the "Dublin Penny Journal," 1833. The most complete, however, of the descriptions previous to the present will be found in Sir W. Wilde's "Beauties of the Boyne and Blackwater," 1847, second edition, 1850; the illustrations, with one exception, are from drawings by Mr. W. F. Wakeman.

The foregoing notices of New Grange do not carry us far, but are definite in some particulars. It is certain that the well-wrought basin, now in the centre of the chamber, was in the east recess, within the basin still there, when the chamber was first entered. I see no sufficient reason for removing it to the centre, and would suggest that it should be restored to its former position. The east recess is the largest and most richly inscribed, and it is more probable that the basin referred to originally stood within the second basin in that recess, as found, than that it was placed there subsequently. In any case we have little more than conjecture to sustain its present position.

New Grange from the air, showing the recent excavations by Prof. M O'Kelly

It is difficult to doubt the positive statement of Lhwyd that a pillar-stone stood on the top of the mound when seen by him. But no trace of this stone existed in 1770, nor has any been found since. The floor of the chamber has been cleared of the loose stones mentioned by Lhwyd, a number of which were placed at the bottom of the pit dug in front of the carved stone at the entrance. They appear to be carefully chosen water-rounded stones, and are of interest as a portion of the original pavement of the chamber, a well-known feature in such structures.

No trace remains of the slender quarry-stone mentioned by Molyneux as lying along the middle of the cave. Molyneux's account is not very reliable, and I am inclined to think no such stone existed: Lhwyd does not mention it, and it is not likely to have been removed. It is possible that the stone which has fallen forward at the right-hand side of the north recess, and which is not unlike that shown on the plan given by Molyneux, may have been confused in his mind as to position. The bones of two dead bodies said to have been found upon the floor are sufficiently accounted for in the "bones of beasts" mentioned by Lhwyd, which in the imagination of the peasantry may have assumed the definite form of "two dead bodies entire." It is not probable that, if any definite information were given as to the finding of human remains, so careful an observer as Lhwyd would have omitted all reference to the matter.

So, far then, do the description of previous writers help us in the restoration of this interesting monument. I fear we must wait for the exploration of some less despoiled tumulus to throw more certain light on the subject.

Many guesses have been hazarded as to the exact use of the stone basins which occupy the recesses. There can hardly be any doubt but that they served the purpose of some rude form of sarcophagus, or of a receptacle for offerings. In the construction of such chambers it is usual to find a sort of sill or low stone placed across the entrance into the main chamber, and at the openings into the smaller chambers or recesses; such stones also occur laid at intervals across the bottom of the passages. This forms a marked feature in the construction at Dowth, and in the cairns on the Loughcrew Hills, but is wholly absent at New Grange. It appears to be further the case that, as a rule, though not invariably so, where stone slabs or basins of large size are found in the sub-chambers, no sill-stone is placed across the entrance.

The use of these basins is probably connected in origin with the mode of burial by inhumation or incineration. They are large enough to hold the body in a contracted position, in which manner, the knees drawn up to the chin, it was not unusually placed. We have no direct evidence as to the mode of burial in the great tumulus at New Grange; but the evidence of other tumuli of apparently the same period and people points to incineration at some time. Wilde mentions that he was present at the opening of a small "Kistvaen" on the western side of the natural slope of the hill of New Grange a few years before he wrote his account of the tumulus: "It was about eight feet long, and consisted of a small stone passage leading into a chamber, formed on the type of the great barrow in that vicinity. In this was discovered a vast collection of the remains of domestic animals, as well as several human bones, some perfect and others in a half-burned state. What gave particular interest to this excavation was the fact of the stones which lined the floor having been vitrified on the external face, which would lead to the conclusion that the cremation had taken place in the grave," He also states that when the tumulus of Dowth was opened by the Royal Irish Academy, in 1847, "within the chamber, mixed with the clay and dust which had accumulated, were found a quantity of bones, consisting of heaps as well as scattered fragments of burned bones, many of which proved to be human." But the evidence of Dowth, as we shall see, owing to a secondary occupation of the chamber, is not reliable. The association of the stone basins referred to with urn burial is, however, strongly supported by Conwell's investigation of the Loughcrew cairns. In the chambers of several of the cairns large quantities of charred human bones, portions of urns, etc., were found. In one cairn (Cairn I.), the chamber contained seven compartments formed of flagstones set on edge. On the floors of five of the latter were placed square flagstones, about 2 feet square by 2 inches thick, On four of these were found charred bones. In another cairn (Cairn L), also containing seven sub-chambers or compartments, stone basins were found on the floors of two of the compartments. The smaller of these measures 2 feet 11 inches by 2 feet, and is hollowed to a depth of about 3 inches: it is confined by a sill-stone. "Mixed with the earth under the sepulchral basin," Conwell says, "were found many fragments of charred bones and several human teeth."

The other basin is of unusual size, measuring 5 feet 9 inches by

"Proceedings R.I.A.," vol. III., p. 262; "Boyne and Blackwater," p. 203.

3 feet 8 inches. The surface of the stone is flat, but surrounded by a raised rim of about an inch in depth, and from two to four inches in breadth; it is not protected by a sill-stone. Mr. Conwell adds that, on raising this stone, pieces of charcoal and upwards of 900 pieces of charred bones were obtained from the earth underneath it; also forty-eight human teeth, two fragments of bone pins, a perfectly rounded syenite ball, two other stone balls, a polished jet-like object, and eight carbonate of lime "brain balls," 154 fragments of rude pottery, and over 1000 portions of bones were collected among the loose stones which filled the chamber of this cairn.

It should be mentioned that the carefully worked basin which stood inside the larger one in the east recess at New Grange is remarkable for the two cup depressions within its hollowed surface. A slightly marked ridge or step is noticeable as dividing the two cups from the central hollow. The two clearly marked cups, 8 and 7 inches in diameter, have given rise to much speculation.

The body of evidence here presented undoubtedly points to incineration as the probable mode of burial in the tumulus of New Grange, or as accompanying the interment of interments. But the question cannot be regarded as settled. The co-existence of a practice of burial of bodies unburned, and after cremation, has been well established in districts of England and in other countries. The occurence of unburnt and burned bodies in the same grave, and under circumstances which place beyond doubt the contemporary nature of the interments, has also been noticed. The subject has not yet been scientifically approached in Ireland, but evidence of a similar character may be found incidentally noticed in our archaeological Journals. Should Knowth prove to be chambered, the opening of this, the third largest of the tumuli in the New Grange group, will probably throw additional light on the subject, unless it should prove to be a cenotaph, but till then we can hardly venture beyond the range of probabilities.

The possibility of other chambers being contained within the great mound of New Grange has been much discussed. The discovery of a second chamber at Dowth would seem to point in that direction. Dowth, I regard, however, as exceptional in that respect, and incline to the opinion that the tumulus at New Grange contains but a single chamber. The fact that the passage and chamber reach but little over one-third within the diameter of

New Grange - part of the interior

the mound is not an exceptional feature, but the usual type of such structures. In the principal cairn on the Loughcrew Hills, the passage and chamber do not extend to even one-third of the diameter. The entrance is clearly marked in the larger of the Loughcrew cairns by the curving inwards of the boundary stones. The entrance at New Grange is similarly marked, and no indication of other chambers is shown on the boundary stones.

Sir Thomas Deane's happy speculation that the spirals on the stone at the back of the west recess were intended as a plan of the mound led to the discovery of two additional carved stones in the boundary circuit, but this I regard as merely a fortunate coincidence, and no trace of passages has been found behind them.

The fact that the chambers generally do not reach more than about one-third the diameter of these large tumuli, is perhaps accounted for in their construction. To raise the roofing-stones into position a sloping embankment of earth was probably necessary. The chamber and passage would, in fact, be erected at one end of an embankment, and the roofing stones brought into place from the back and sides. In completing the mound, it would naturally be raised on the dimensions of the embankment already used for the purpose of bringing the stones into position, and the chamber would consequently lie towards the circumference. To preserve access to a chamber placed in the centre of a mound of the dimensions of New Grange would necessitate a passage of some 130 feet in length. Now, as the height of the mound depends on the diameter of the base, unless the passage be thus unduly prolonged, height must be obtained by an extension of the base at the back of the chamber. The chamber and passage having been constructed, the desire to mark the importance of the monument by the height of the mound will, therefore, naturally lead to an extension of the base to the back, and consequent displacing of the chamber from the centre of the mound.

One other feature of interest in reference to the construction of the tumulus may be mentioned. Wilde states that the stones of which the tumulus is constructed in some cases belong to a class of rock not found in the neighbourhood; some, he adds, are basaltic, and others must have been transported from the Mourne Mountains.

Mr. R. Clark of the Geological Survey, who accompanied me on the occasion of one visit to New Grange, has kindly furnished the following short report on this point:—

"Both these remarkable structures, Dowth and New Grange, are erected on the drift which in this neighbourhood thickly covers the coal measures formation. The passages and chambers of the two mounds have been formed of large slabs of the Lower Silurian rocks which crop up within a few miles' distance. They were apparently either rudely quarried for the purpose or split from surface rocks. With the exception of some of the stones in the passage and others of the upright course, the slabs in the interior of New Grange show little traces of the original weathered surface of the rocks from which they were taken, but, on the contrary, even faces, which indicate that they have been split along the cleavage, and care taken in their selection. The spiral carvings have been cut exclusively on this description of stone; and, considering the exposed positions of the external slabs, they show but little effect of weathering. Each mound is surrounded by a circle of elongated blocks and slabs placed on the edge. These also are mostly derived from the Silurian rocks, interspersed with a few varieties of traps. The parent rocks of the latter are probably to be found amongst the igneous rocks which are associated with the Silurian beds in the vicinity of the neighbouring town of Slane. In the outer circle at New Grange are a number of standing stones, mainly of Silurians (grits and slates); a few traps also occur which may also be referred to the Slane district. The large standing stone near the River Boyne, at New Grange, is composed of a fine compact grit. In the centre of the chamber of the New Grange structure is a granite basin, which Wilkinson in his 'Ancient Architecture of Ireland' states to be of Mourne origin. It is difficult, owing to the defective light to be obtained, to definitely fix the locality from which the material for this basin was procured. To the writer it appeared to bear more resemblance to some of the granites of the Wicklow series than to those of the Mourne district.

"There is no doubt that with the exception of the granite basin above referred to all the materials used were procurable within a radius of a few miles. Wilkinson points out in his work that flags of very considerable size can be obtained in a quarry at the old gateway of Melifont Abbey: it is not improbable that this was the source from which the huge slabs at Dowth and New Grange were obtained."

Wilde's statement appears, therefore, to be too general. Basalt is found at Slane, within a distance of three or four miles; and the granite basin is the only stone the presence of which is difficult to account for. The fact that the stones are local reduces little our estimate of the labour expended on the construction of New Grange. To convey stones of such great size even a few miles must have proved a task of no ordinary difficulty. Whether the granite be referred to the Mourne or to the Wicklow district, if it has not been conveyed to its present locality by natural agencies, would imply carriage of over fifty miles. The dimensions of the basin, about 4 feet by 3 feet 6 in., by 1 foot thick, are, however, more manageable than most of the blocks of the structure, and reduce the difficulties of transport.

The remarkable carvings on the stones of the passage and chamber at New Grange have afforded a wide field for conjecture.

Pownall saw in one of the markings Phoenician character. Colonel Vallancey constructed an alphabet from them, and read the name Angus. The veteran archaeologist, Sir R. C. Hoare, rejected such fancies. In his "Tour in Ireland," p. 256, he observes: "Some antiquarians have carried their zeal so far as to discover (in idea) letters on the stones, which they have attributed to the Phoenicians; whilst others have denominated them *Ogham* characters: those marks which I have observed on many of the stones bore very little resemblance to letters, and a great similarity to the ornaments I have found on the ancient British urns discovered under our tumuli in Wiltshire."

The valuable suggestion here thrown out fell unnoticed. Sir W. Wilde says, in "The Boyne and the Blackwater," "The question may well be asked, what was their purpose? are they mere ornamental carvings, or are they inscriptions from which the history of this monument, or whatever it was originally intended for, might be learned? Are they ideographical, or hierographic, in the strict sense of that word, that is, sacred carvings? To this latter we are inclined; and if we may be allowed to coin a word to express our meaning, we would call them Tymboglyphics, or *tomb-writings*, for similar characters have as yet only been found connected with the vestiges of ancient sepulchres, as here at Dowth, and on tombs of a like character in the counties of Down and Donegal."

I have held the opinion for some time that the conditions of the inscribings at New Grange are satisfied by those of ornament—that, in fact, these markings simply represent the style of decoration of the period, and that their explanation is to be chiefly sought in that direction. It is probable that some of the figures were on their origin symbolical; but we must distinguish between essential meaning and constructive meaning. The spiral may be used symbolically, but it is not necessary to see in every spiral symbolical meaning. I hope to show, in the succeeding pages, that in treatment and position the carvings in New Grange are used with a decorative end, and, though the delight of mystery may be thus removed, to establish the added importance of this great monument as marking the beginning of decorative art and architecture in Ireland.

The New Grange inscribings are commonly classed with those at Dowth and Loughcrew. But important distinctions must be made. Thus, whereas many of the stones at New Grange are cup-marked, not a single example is found of cup-and-ring marks, which are found at Loughcrew, or of concentric circles found at the latter and at Dowth. Where the circle with concentric curves occurs, it is used in combination to form a new figure; it is never used in isolation simply as concentric circles, as at Dowth and Loughcrew.

New Grange after excavation and restoration

LITERARY REFERENCES

The Plates will show the nature of the recesses, also some of the inscribed stones. The probable origin and meaning of the inscribed marks will be discussed in future chapters, when the position of all the inscribed and other noticeable stones will be described.

Before proceeding further with the archaeology of the inscribed stone-markings in detail, it may be best, however, to give a brief account of some of the references to the Brugh in the ancient literature of Ireland, as showing the fame as well as the general extent of the cemetery. They show how the district was regarded through centuries as the chief burial-place for the Kings of Tara. The principal mounds were probably visited on ceremonial occasions and yearly festivals. This is indicated in the passages concerning Knowth, and may explain certain difficulties in regarding all the markings on a stone as made at the one time.

The more important tracts relating to *Brugh na Boinne,* or *Brugh* as it is generally called, have been translated. *Brugh* usually signifies a mansion, palace, or "burg"; it is also used in a wider sense to signify land, plain, town. (See W. M. Hennessy's introduction to the Mesca Ulad, or the Intoxication of the Ultonians.) Many of the incidental references are also accessible. We thus possess substantially the whole body of the evidence bearing on the question of the identification of the cemetery.

The incidental references are, for the most part, of a fabulous character, and refer to the association of Aengus, son of the Dagda, with *Brugh na Boinne.* Thus in the *Pursuit of Diarmuid and Grainne,* on the death of Diarmuid, Finn says: "Let us leave this tulach, for fear that Aengus-an-Bhrogha and the Tuatha De Danaan might catch us; and though we have no part in the slaying of Diarmuid, he would none the more readily believe us." It is then related how Aengus came and took the body of Diarmuid to the Brugh on the Boyne, saying, "Since I cannot restore him to life, I will send a soul into him, so that he may talk to me each day." Many other examples of a similar character might be given, but one other, to which my friend Dr. Douglas Hyde has drawn my attention, will be sufficient. In the Fenian story, the Bruighion Chaorthainn, or ford of the Rowan-tree, of which several manuscript copies of the last century and of the early part of the present century exist, it is related how, on a certain occasion, a poet brought four ranns or stanzas to Finn, and offered to take as payment for the poem the complete understanding of it. And he put Finn under *geasa* to understand it. The first of these ranns, and Finn's answer, Dr. Hyde translates thus: —

> "I saw a house in the country
> Out of which no hostages are given to a king,
> Fire burns it not, harrying spoils it not:
> Good the prosperity with which was conceived
> the kingly house."

"I understand that verse," said Finn, "for that is the Brugh of the Boyne that you have seen, namely, the house of Aengus Og of the Brugh, and it cannot be burned or harried as long as Aengus shall live, so there's the explanation of that verse for you," said Finn, "True," said the youth, etc.

These are, of course, of no historical value, but are not without interest as evidence of the persistence of the traditional association of the great mound at New Grange with *Brugh na Boinne,* and the natural centering of the later growths in the myth of Aengus round that mound as the most important monument in the district. O'Donovan, in a note to the "Four Masters" (p. 22), states that "Aengus-an-Bhrogha was considered the presiding fairy of the Boyne till recently, and that his name is still familiar to the old inhabitants of Meath. . . ."

The detailed mention of Brugh in the Senchus na Relic, or History of the Cemetries, of the "Leabhar na hUidhri," and in the Dindsenchus, deserves more serious attention. The prose portion of the History of the Cemeteries and the prose passages relating to our subject in the Dindsenchus were translated by O'Donovan for Petrie, and are published, with the Irish text, in the latter's "Round Towers of Ireland."

The "Leabhar na h-Uidhri" is a compilation of the twelfth or probably of the end of the eleventh century, and is the earliest of the Irish manuscripts of a non-ecclesiastical character at present in existence. It was compiled at Clonmacnoise by Moelmuiri, whose death is recorded in the annals under the year 1106. The tract on the cemeteries is to be referred to a period probably some centuries earlier. It is glossed by Moelmuiri, and his explanations are given within brackets in the translation in Petrie's "Round Towers of Ireland," p. 100.

It is a long tract, but it is unnecessary to give it in full. The following passages will be sufficient for the present purposes. I have gone into the whole question in much detail in the Trans.

R.I.A., vol xxx, pp. 73–92, to which readers are referred:—

"... The nobles of the Tuatha De Danann were used to bury at Brugh, (i.e., the Dagda with his three sons; also Lugaidh, and Oe, and Ollam, and Ogma, and Etan, the Poetess, and Corpre, the son of Etan), and Cremhthann followed them because his wife Nar was of the Tuatha Dea, and it was she solicited him that he should adopt Brugh as a burial-place for himself and his descendants, and this was the cause that they did not bury at Cruachan...."

The passages referring to Brugh are then certified by a poem of twenty-two stanzas ascribed to Cinaeth O'Hartagain (d. 973), beginning: *an sin a maig mic ind oc*. It particularizes the monuments of the notable persons interred at Brugh, after the manner of the prose lists in the "Book of Ballymote," to be given presently. The first line of the eighth stanza, *Sechi bo boadain buain,* which seems to refer to the existence of a monument at Brugh to Boadan, is of importance, and will be referred to again. The fifteenth stanza tells the burial-place of Cormac:—

> "He took station over the white Boyne,
> On the strand at *Ross na righ.*"

Ros na Righ, still known by that name (Rosnaree), is situated on the opposite bank of the Boyne, about half a mile above New Grange. Cormac's grave is still pointed out there; O'Donovan, however, does not consider the tradition to have been handed down, but derived from Comerford's History of Ireland. (Ordnance Letters, R.I.A., "Meath-Antiquities," p. 279).

The following prose commentary—on a poem ascribed to Dorban—apparently written by Moelmuiri, concludes the tract:—

"The chiefs of Ulster before Conchobor were buried at Talten, viz., Ollamh Fodhla and seven of his sons, and grandsons, with others of the chiefs of Ulster. The nobles of the Tuatha De Danann (with the exception of seven of them who were interred at Talten) were buried at Brugh, i.e. Lugh, and Oe, son of Ollamh, and Ogma, and Carpre, son of Etan, and Etan [the poetess] herself, and the Dagda and his three sons (i.e. Aedh, and Oengus, and Cermait), and a great many others besides of the Tuatha De Dannanns, and Firbolgs, and others. The kings of the province of Galian [Leinster] *were buried* at Oenach Ailbi; the kings of Munster at Oenach Culi, in Oenach Colman and Feci. The Clann Dedhadh at Temhair Erann. The kings of Connaught at Cruachan *ut diximus.*

"There are fifty hills [mounds] at each Oenach of these: fifty hills at Oenach Cruachan, fifty hills at Oenach Talten, and fifty at Oenach in Broga." ....

The "Book of Ballymote," a manuscript of the fourteenth century (1391), is, like the "Leabhar na hUidhri," a compilation

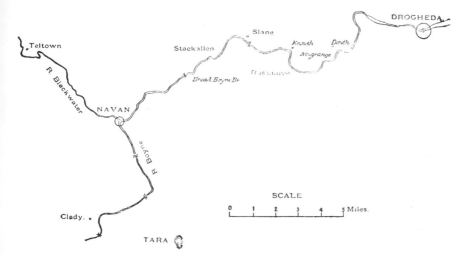

Fig 3

from older sources. The following passage from the "Dindsenchus"
sets forth the principal monuments at Brugh:—

"Of the monuments at Brugh her, viz., the Bed of the daughter
of Forann, the Monument of the Dagda, the Mound of the
Morrigan, the Monument of [the monster] Mata: it is from its
colpa, or thigh, Inbher Colptha is called: the *Barc* of Crimthann
Nianar, in which he was interred; the grave of Fedelmidh, the
Lawgiver, the *Carn-ail* [stone carn] of Conn of the Hundred
Battles, the *Cumot* [commensurate grave] of Cairbre Lifeachair,
the *Fulacht* of Fiacha Sraiphtine."

Text and translation of extract in Petrie's "Round Towers," p. 102.

Then follows a second prose passage in which the monuments
of the Brugh are set forth in greater detail, into which we need not
enter.

In the foregoing extracts we find a mixture of mythical and
dimly historical persons, into particulars about whom we need not
go. Their importance in the present connexion consists in that
they establish the existence at a very early date of tradition
associating Brugh na Boinne, the burial-place of the Kings of Tara,
with the tumuli on the Boyne, Without attaching particular weight
to the statements concerning Art and Cormac, and the reasons
why they were not interred at Brugh, we may at least infer that
the district of Brugh was used for the Kings of Tara until the
introduction of Christianity, and that it was then abandoned. The
association of particular monuments with the Dagda and other
divinities and heroes of Irish mythology implies that the actual
persons for whom they were erected had been forgotten. The
mythical ancestors of the heroes and kings interred at Brugh, who,
probably, were even contemporarily associated with the cemetery,
no doubt subsequently overshadowed in tradition the actual
persons interred there.

It will be remembered that one of the "caves" mentioned in the "annals," as among those plundered in the ninth century, is described as "the cave of Boadan over Dubadh" (Dowth). The reference to Boadan in Cineath O'Hartagain's poem may therefore be said to settle the question of the inclusion of Dowth with Brugh. And a further reference in the "Book of Leinster," connecting Knowth with Brugh, is conclusive as to the identity of the monuments under consideration with that cemetery.

The reference to Boadan in O'Hartagains's poem may be recalled, and the passage in the "Book of Leinster" connecting Knowth with Brugh brought forward.

As already mentioned, the Boyne tumuli were plundered by the Danes in the ninth century. In the "Annals of Ulster" the incident is recorded, under the year 862, in these words:—

"The cave of Achadh-Aldai, and [the cave] of Cnodhba, and the cave of Fort-Boadan over Dubadh, and the cave of the smith's wife, were searched by the foreigners, *quod antea non perfectum est*, viz. on the occasion when three kings of the foreigners plundered the land of Flann, son of Conaing, to wit, Amhlaim, and Imhar, and Auisle; and Lorcan, son of Cathal, king of Meath, was with them thereat."

The Field of Aldai. —*An ancestor of the Tuatha De Danann. —MacFirbis' Genealogies.*

Elcmar. —*One of the Tuatha De Danann— Elcmhair-an-Bhroga. — MacFirbis.*

Drogheda.

In the "Annals of the Four Masters" the same incident is recorded under the year 861, thus:—

"Amhlaeibh, Imhar, and Uailsi, three chieftains of the foreigners; and Lorcan, son of Cathal, Lord of Meath, plundered the land of Flann, son of Conang. The cave of Achadh-Aldai, in Mughdhorna-Maighen; the cave of Cnoghbhai; the cave of the grave of Bodan, i.e. the shepherd of Elemar, over Dubhath; and the cave of the wife of Gobhann, at Drochat-atha, were plundered by the same foreigners."

O'Donovan, note to the "Four Masters," p. 496.

Mugdhorna-Maigen appears to be a mistake of transcription for Mughdhorna-Breagh. The caves plundered were in one territory, namely, in the land of Flann, son of Conang, one of the chieftains of Meath. Whereas Mughdhorna-Maigen is in Oriel, many miles north of the land of Flann.

The reference to Knowth in the "Book of Leinster" is more definite; it occurs in a poem containing the Dindsenchus of Naas ascribed to Mac Nia. This poem is also preserved in the Books of Ballymote and Hy Maine, where it is preceded by the usual prose account. The prose Dindsenchus of Naas, as given in the "Book of Ballymote," concludes thus:—

"*Nas* now was mother of *Ibich*, son of *Lugh*, and it was here *Nas* died and was buried, hence *Nas* it is called. Her sister then died at once of grief for her, namely, *Bui*, and was buried in *Cnoc baea*, unde *Cnogba* dicitur, i.e. *Cnoc-Bua*. *Lugh* convened the hosts of Gaidels with him from *Tailtiu* to Fiadh mBroga to mourn those women on the Kalends of August in every year, and hence *Nasadh Luga*, unde *Lugnassadh*, i.e. the *Conarc Loga* or the commemoration, or the anniversary, or the vigil of death, de quibus hoc carmen dicitur."

This passage is certified by Mac Nia's poem, the following extracts from which are quoted from the "Book of Leinster" as the more ancient authority. In the last line of the second stanza Bui is called Bui of the Brugh—*bui in broga*. The poem then gives the origin of the name Nas, as in the prose account, and proceeds:—

> "Her sister at *Cnogba* . . .
> It is there Bui was buried."

The next stanza but one contains a further reference to Brugh, which completes the chain of evidence:—

> "Hosts of fair Gaedel came
> to mourn the women to the Brugh
> from Tailtui . . . . ."

The foregoing extracts scarcely need comment. Not only in direct statement, but in the reference to Bui as "Bui of the Brugh," the traditional association of Knowth with Brugh is definitely established.

Irish Text given in my original Memoir, Trans. R.I.A., vol. xxx.

However, in an unfinished copy of the Dindsenchus in the Bodleian Library there is a different account of the origin of the name Cnogba ascribed to the end of the fourteenth, or beginning of the fifteenth, century.

"Englic, daughter of Elcmaire, loved Oengus mac ind Oc, and she had not seen him. They held a meeting for games there between Cletech and Sid in Broga. The Bright Folk and fairy hosts of Ireland used to visit that game every Hallowe'en, having a moderate share of food, to wit, a nut. From the north went three sons of Derc, son of Ethaman, out of Sid Findabrach, and they eloped with Elemaire's daughter (going) round the young folk without their knowledge. When they knew it, they ran after her as far as the hill named Cnogba. Great lamentation they made there,

Sid, or sidh, was anciently applied to a hill or mound, the interior of which was supposed to be inhabited by fairy folk, who were called side *(pron. shee-e). It appears also to have meant 'a caved hill,' and is considered to signify 'a burial-place.' See Hennessy's Introduction to "Mesca Ulad," Todd Lectures, vol. i., Int., p. vi. See also Rhys, "Hibbert Lectures," 1886, p. 147.*

and this is the feast that supported them, their gathering. Hence 'Cnogba,' that is cno-guba, 'nut lamentation,' from the lamentation they made at yon gathering.

> Hence is Cnogba of the troops,
> So that every host deems it famous,
> From the lamentation after reaping nuts . . .
> Following Elcmair's daughter."

See text and traslation by Whitley Stokes, in "Folk-Lore," vol. iii., p. 506.

Reviewing the evidence as a whole, I think it will be apparent that the error which led to seeking the site of Brugh at Stackallen was from the necessity of distinguishing Brugh from the New Grange tumuli, from the restricted signification that appears to have been attached to Brugh, which it was sought to identify with some particular place on the Boyne, rather than as applied to a district of some extent. From the references in the manuscripts, especially in the poems, it is clear that the cemetery covered a considerable space of ground. The existing remains, from Cloghalea to Knowth, extend over a distance of about three miles, and agree closely in character with the general description of the monuments in the "Senchus na Relic" and "Dindsenchus," consisting of mounds, raths, and pillar-stones. It was on this ground that Wilde, taking a common-sense view of the question, rejected the conjectural site of Stackallen. The New Grange group of tumuli was probably the most important portion of the cemetery, and there, probably, was the place of assembly with which the great rath at Dowth was possibly connected. But how far beyond these limits the district known as Brugh may have extended we do not know. About a mile and a half north of the mound of New Grange a small caved tumulus is marked on the Ordnance Map, and a couple of miles above Slane another "moat," as these artificial mounds are called, is marked, which may also be sepulchral. Many lesser graves have probably been destroyed or cannot now be traced.

The passages concerning Nas seem to indicate an annual ceremony or sacred meeting taking place at Knowth, a vigil of the dead and feast of nut-gathering. How far these myths go back we cannot say. The literary accounts could not have been put into shape until more than a thousand years after the erection of the monuments, and the myth had grown to explain the sites, so little can be based on them but they may contain some survival of the ceremonies paid to the original dead, though we must not assume a continuity of tribe or nation.

Concerning the sacred rites of the dead, the late Mr. Borlase collected many passages, from which these and their survival may be inferred. A long note in the "Dolmens of Ireland," p.345, vol. ii, may be read with much interest.

Plate III Entrance to New Grange

ART AT NEW GRANGE

We may now resume the discussion of the inscribed stones at New Grange. They were first all published in my original memoir from drawings and photographs; but since then they have been cast for the Museum in 1901; and I shall use photographs from the casts chiefly for the present work.

Taking those in the chamber first, and proceeding from left to right, we find in the left or west recess three spirals on the back stone, the principal one of which is especially large and good (fig. 4); and on the left side stone one large spiral, above which are five lozenges (fig. 5). Over this on a long stone are a row of nine lozenges and some eleven or twelve chevrons (fig. 6).

Fig 4

Fig 5

The stone on the right side of the recess has the famous marking which has excited the guesses of so many antiquaries.

Some doubts have been expressed as to the genuineness of this marking. It existed, however, prior to 1770, when it was figured in the "Archaeologia"; and the discovery of a similar figure on one of the stones of a tumulus at Locmariaker, in Brittany, conclusively establishes its authenticity. Governor Pownall concluded that the characters were Phoenician, but only numerals. Fergusson is of the opinion that it can hardly be a mere ornament, but must be either a mason's mark or recognizable symbol of some sort, something to

Fig 6

mark the position of the stone or its ownership by some person. Similar marks, he adds, are found in France, but seem equally devoid of any recognizable meaning. He compares it with that referred to at Locmariaker, which it closely resembles.

There is no doubt that the marking at New Grange is a rude representation of a ship or galley similar to those of the Scandinavian rock-tracings.

The large carved blocking stone at the entrance to New Grange

Fig 7

Fig 8

The Scandinavian rock-tracings furnish conclusive evidence as to the meanings of the markings referred to on the Locmariaker stones, and to establish that they are representations of boats, and therefore that the rude sculpturing at New Grange represents also a ship or galley. I have noted this point at some length in the original memoir; but it need not here be discussed at such length, as it is now generally accepted; fig. 7 will show it sufficiently. There is a small circle over the ship. In the rock-tracings the ships are represented with and without men.

On the edge face of the stone projecting into the chamber is the well-known fern-leaf or palm-branch (fig. 8). The drawing of the leaf is very naturalistic. The lower part of the branch, however, partakes of the conventional character of the herring-bone or, as it is some-times called, tree-pattern. To the left at the base of the branch are a row of small chevrons which may indicate water from which the branch springs, and add to its general resemblance to a fern or palm-branch.

Passing around the chamber there is nothing of interest save an occasional cup-mark until we come to the north recess. One stone has fallen a little forward; it shows three good spirals combined to make a form of three. If we follow out its lines, we find it consists of two double spirals joined S-wise, with a third returning spiral added at the left-hand side, the loose ends of which are carried round the other two, but are structurally independent of them. Above this are a row of halved lozenges and triangles faintly marked (fig. 9): the way the picking has been begun at the top disposes of any doubt as to their genuineness.

Behind this a stone in the walling was until recently partly exposed; but it has lately been built up, and can no longer be seen. The spirals inscribed on the under-surface of this stone were disclosed by the falling out of several of the stones which formed the wallpacking.

The fine fresh carving of the spirals is shown in the drawing I made when the stone was partly exposed (fig. 10). We pass now to the east recess.

This was evidently the principal recess or chamber both on account of its greater depth and somewhat chamber-like construction. It was here that the basin now in the centre of the chamber originally stood, inside the present larger one. The large slab which forms the roof of this chamber has many figures on the exposed surface, of spirals; a figure of a lozenge surrounded by

Fig 9

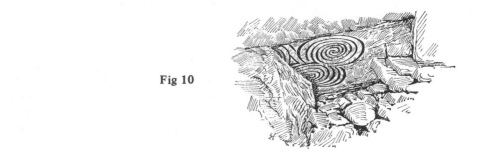

Fig 10

Plate IV New Grange - the left recess of the chamber

New Grange - one of the decorated stones

New Grange - the left recess of the chamber

eight circles enclosed in a scolloped border of concentric curves, and other marks, cover the entire face of the stone. See Plate VII, also an old cast taken by R.I.A. (fig. 11).

At the back of the recess is a stone with bold chevrons ending in some picked triangles or lozenges towards the right end; it is much flaked in parts (fig. 12). Along the right side towards the top is a stone with a row of six plain lozenges (fig. 13). They are all clearly marked out and picked to some depth.

Fig 11

Fig 13

Fig 12

Outside this recess one of the two great stones which form it, and give it an architectural appearance, is picked with some lozenges and triangles towards the top of the stone (fig. 14).

On the edge of a stone over the opening of the passage into the chamber are some triangles or halved lozenges (fig. 15).

We have now passed round the chamber, and save for an occasional cup-mark have noticed all the inscribed markings appearing on it.

Several stones in the passage require special notice; they are all numbered on the plan, the numbers being on both right and left sides counted from the entrance. The first stone in the passage going out of the chamber is very remarkable. This great stone has six ribs hollowed out across it. The skin or surface of the stone has been picked nearly all over, including the ribs. If these were in the first-instance obtained by friction, they were subsequently picked; and Sir William Wilde is incorrect in speaking of these grooves as smooth. Below the ribs there is a deep cup sunk somewhat oval in form; there are some small cups on the edge of the stone; and near the top several half lozenges are incised. (Fig. 16)

Fig 16

New Grange - the chamber looking towards the end recess

The design on the stone No. 20, on the opposite side, has been treated in the same way. In this instance the ground has been picked so as to leave the pattern of the chevrons in relief; but some attempt has been made to strike a line round the design, and outside the panel thus formed, the greater part of the surface of the stone has been picked over. The process was not apparently completed; large patches of the skin remain on the right-hand side of the stone. (Fig. 17)

Fig 17

49

Plate VI New Grange - the right recess

New Grange - the main chamber showing the triple spiral on an upright. *See Fig 9*

On close examination it will be found that the majority of the unornamented stones, as well as those bearing devices, have been similarly treated; in some cases the entire surface has been carefully picked over, and the skin completely removed; in others, patches of the water worn or weathered surface remain. Stone No. 10, on the left side of the passage, affords an excellent illustration of this; the skin has been removed over about half its surface; and on the remaining portion a number of pick-marks are noticeable, showing where the process had been begun.

Number 17 on the left side, is one of the most famous stones; it has frequently been illustrated. It contains three spirals surrounding a lozenge, and above these some well-marked chevrons. These markings were all that were known when the stone was previously illustrated; but at the time the stone was cast, the lower portion was brought to light; this shows four spirals, two large and two

Fig 18

small joined in pairs, and some chevrons below them. It looks as if the lower markings had been partly obliterated by the picking, which is very clear on the stone, and goes over most of the lower spirals (Fig. 19)

Fig 19

Plate VII Roofing stone of right recess

Left and below : Decorated
stones at New Grange

Fig 22 Stone over entrance

Fig 20

Fig 21

Stone No. 19, on the right, is incised with some good chevrons; but the remarkable thing about it is that the markings are quite obliterated on the right half; they may have been taken off by a chisel; but whether a bronze or iron tool was used we cannot say. The marks are about the width of an ordinary bronze chisel. The chisel has been driven sideways; and the marks are quite different from the pick-marks already referred to. They are about three-quarters of an inch long by half an inch broad, and in each cut the marks left by the gapped edge of the chisel are quite distinct. The edge of bronze tools appears to get worn if used for such a purpose, and this would have shown in the cuts, which are very distinct; but the surface of this stone is not very hard, and a bronze tool may have been capable of removing it. (Fig. 20)

Stone No. 20, right, has an oval hollow in which some circles lie; it bears some resemblance to the markings on the outer stone at *a* on Plan. (Fig. 21)

Stone No. 21, left, is an excellent illustration of the picking already mentioned; the skin has been removed over about half its surface; and on the remaining portion a number of pick-marks are noticeable, showing where the process had been begun.

The ribbed stone has been already referred to (fig. 16). Another instance occurs on stone No. 12, on the same side, on which three similar grooves are cut; and on the left side of the passage, stone No. 11 is noticeable for a single vertical groove. In all these cases the grooves, if formed by rubbing, have been afterwards picked.

Stone No. 12, right, has on the side which faces the next stone some scarcely noticeable triangles picked.

Stone No. 13, left, has a row of three well-marked lozenges inscribed on it. They are similarly treated to those on the great stone; but in this case the lozenges are quartered (fig. 18).

I have now noticed all the interesting stones in the passage; there only remain four stones outside to be mentioned, which complete the carved stones of New Grange. A notable stone is one over the entrance. The ornament, of saltire form, is cut in relief on the projecting edge of the stone, and fitly marks its horizontal course; and in the lines cut on its upper face a remarkable approximation towards a moulding is shown of a distinctly architectural character (fig. 22.) This instance, however rudimentary in character, taken in connexion with the remarkable enterprise shown in the roofing of the chamber, appears to me of much significance, and to indicate architectural promptings of much interest.

The stone across the entrance is the best known of the series; it is carved with spirals, the loose ends of which are carried round in concentric circles so as to group the three principal spirals together. Lozenges fill the end portions of this stone. (See Plate III.)

Close view of the carving illustrated in Fig 19

The two stones mentioned in the boundary circle (Plan *a* and *b*) are the best examples of carving in relief. Figs 23 and 24 show them. I shall return to them later.

Fig 23 Stone *a* on plan

Fig 24 Stone *b* on plan

One other point of interest deserves to be mentioned in connexion with the inscribed stones. Sir William Wilde was struck by a remarkable circumstance when investigating the tumulus. In "The Boyne and the Blackwater," he says he found that the carvings, "not only covered portions of the stones exposed to view, but extended over those surfaces which, until some recent dilapidation, were completely concealed from view, and where a tool could not have reached them." And he adds: "The inference is plain, that these stones were carved prior to their being placed in their present position; perhaps were used for some anterior purpose. If so, how much it adds to their antiquity!"

Figure 11 is the most striking instance in point. The spirals inscribed on the under surface of this stone have been disclosed by the falling out of several of the stones which formed the packing. Some triangles picked on the under surface of the stone near the projecting edge are omitted in the drawing. The carving of the roof-stone of the east recess also extends beyond the portion of the stone exposed, and is partly concealed by the stones on which it rests. This feature would be remarkable, and afford occasion for interesting speculation, were it peculiar to New Grange; but it appears to be usual in such structures. It occurs at Loughcrew. In the description of the roofing-stone of the western chamber of the principal tumulus on the Loughcrew hills, Conwell says: "Above the upright stones forming its walls are observed seven projecting flags, forming a beehive roof, capped by a large horizontal flag elaborately covered with devices, several of which extend out of sight under the structure, and where no tool could reach; again affording evidence that the sculptures upon this stone also must have been executed before the erection of the carn."

The same feature is found in the tumulus of Gavr'inis in Brittany. In 1884 Dr. de Closmadeuc had some of the stones of the flooring of that remarkable structure raised, and found that the edge-face of one of these stones was inscribed. The carving on some of the wall-stones was also found to extend below the floor; and the side-faces of some of these stones were carved. The investigations brought to light carvings which had remained hidden up to then, and established the fact that the blocks were prepared and sculptured before being placed in position.

Wilde mentions a point in connexion with the carving on the stone (fig. 10) which he appears to have recognized as rather telling against the supposition that these carved stones were used for some anterior purpose. The flag in question has, as he remarks, "a sort of skin, or brownish outer polish, as if water-washed. Now in all the exposed carvings on the other stones, the indentures have assumed more or less of the dark colour and polish around; whereas in this one the colour of the cutting and the track of the tool is just as fresh as if done yesterday. It must have been effected immediately before the stone was placed in its present position."

The explanation of the apparent anomaly in the concealment of portions of the carvings is, perhaps, not far to seek. It is evident from the positions of many of the stones, such as the roof-stone of the east recess, apart from other considerations, that the majority of the stones must have been carved before being placed in their present positions. Again, the stones could hardly have been carved in the dark, or with the artificial light at the disposal of the builders. All the circumstances of convenience point to the carving of the stones before erection.

We do not draw much on imagination if we assume as the probable course of construction that the stones were first collected on the site, and were, in many instances, carved on the spot without definite reference to the position they would occupy in the structure. The builders appear to have endeavoured, as far as possible, to display the carved portions of the stones; but it is probable that in some cases the stones were found suitable for positions in which it was not possible to do so, and the decoration was sacrificed to the needs of construction. In working in stone, they would be led by artistic habit, as in the carving of a spear-shaft, to look on the stone as the final repository of the ornament, and would hardly consider its relation to the structure; an advance in art which would come later, and would, in fact, denote a more defined conception of architecture than we find in the monument —though the first promptings of architectural art may be recognized in its construction and disposal of ornament.

DOWTH AND OTHER TUMULI

Fig 25 Standing-stone *C* on map

In the next field, about 80 yards to the west of the great mound, two slight rises are noticeable in the slope of the ground, on the farthest of which are the remains of a small tumulus. Wilde describes it as "about 8 feet long, and consisting of a small stone passage leading into a little chamber, formed on the type of the great barrow in that vicinity." This is not quite correct. The chamber seems to have been square, and the passage somewhat longer than Wilde's estimate. The circle of this small tumulus appears to be about 35 feet in diameter. The second rise, a few yards nearer the mound, may perhaps have been the site of a cairn, judging from the position and a few loose stones on the top, but they may be simply field-stones.

In the fields adjoining the great tumulus at New Grange, some smaller tumuli deserve notice before proceeding to the mound at Dowth.

Below the great mound of New Grange two well-defined tumuli may be seen showing as conical grass-covered hillocks on the low-lying land by the river. They are marked A and B on map. "A" is 220 feet in circumference and about 20 feet high; "B" 300 feet in circumference and about the same height. The measurements are approximate. "A" appears to have been encircled, at a distance of about 200 feet from the mound, by a vallum, a portion of which is still traceable at the east side. These mounds have probably been plundered, but are at present evenly grass-grown.

On the brow of the steep bank which rises at some distance behind these grave-mounds a great block of compact sandstone grit has been set on end, and forms a most remarkable standing-stone ("C"), similar to, but larger than, those set round the great mound. It measures 10 feet high, and is 17 feet in girth (fig. 25). In the adjoining field a similar standing-stone will be found; but it is not so large. In the field to the left are several large stones (see map), probably the remains of some sepulchral monument. At the top of the next field is one of the most remarkable of the lesser tumuli, marked "E" on map. Its base is enclosed by a well-defined circle of boundary stones. It measures about 280 feet in circumference and 12 feet in height.

Walking across the fields towards Dowth we pass the mounds "F," "G," "H" on map. The long mound "G" is of unusual shape; it is about 150 feet in length by 60 in width and 10 high. From the depressions in the surfaces of these mounds we may conclude that they have been plundered. At the far side of the great mound of Dowth, in the grounds at the back of Dowth House, are two smaller tumuli ("I" and "J"), one of which is open from the top. The centre of the latter consists of a corbel-roofed chamber, formed of flags laid on the plan of an irregular hexagon. The chamber thus formed is about 8 feet high and 10 feet in diameter. Five cells are placed round the sides, formed by small flags set on edge; no trace of a passage is apparent; none of the stones are inscribed.

In Dowth demesne, in the same field as the great ring-fort—said to be the second largest in Ireland—at a place marked Cloughlea on map, Wilde mentions there being "a portion of a stone circle, evidently a part of the side-wall or basement of a sepulchral chamber similar to New Grange." "Human remains have," he adds, "on more than one occasion been found in the vicinity of this remnant of an ancient tumulus."

When Pownall saw this circle, eleven stones were in position. He says:—"I paced this circle, and, as well as I recollect it, it is not above 21 feet. The stones are large and massive, and about 5 and 6 feet high. There remain eight of these stones together in one part of the circle; two in another part, and one by itself. On the left hand from the entrance into the circle lies a large flat stone, which seems to have been either the top of a kistvaen or a cromlech."

The remains of this monument are still to be seen, though I could not make out all the stones mentioned.

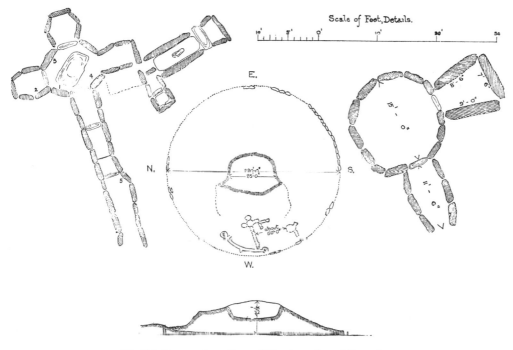

Fig 26 Plan and section of the tumulus at Dowth

The great tumulus at Dowth appears to have been about the same size as that at New Grange, and agrees closely in its present measurements with the latter. It averages in height about 47 feet, and 280 feet in diameter. The base is surrounded by a curb of large stones set on edge at New Grange; but it is not encircled by any retaining wall. No trace of an outside circle of standing-stones exists, nor are any found at Knowth. New Grange would appear in this respect, as in others, exceptional, and was no doubt the most important monument in the group. The plans and sections (fig. 26), based on those published by Sir Thomas Deane in the Proceedings R.I.A., 3rd Ser., vol. ii., but with additional measurements, will show the general features of the mound and chambers at Dowth.

It is not known when the entrance to the tumulus was discovered. Previous to its exploration by a committee of the Royal Irish Academy in 1847, a considerable gap, Wilde says, existed in the western face of the mound, caused by stones having been removed for buildings or macadamizing materials for the adjoining road. In this excavation a passage somewhat similar to that at New Grange had long been exposed, but is was not possible to follow it for more than a few yards on either side. "Whether," he adds, "this passage was that originally broken open by Amlaff and his plundering Danes it is difficult to determine."

Unfortunately no official record exists of the exploration of the tumulus by the Royal Irish Academy. Plans and drawings appear to have been made, but no trace of them can now be found. Indeed, the mound was so pulled about by the explorers, and the work carried out with such doubtful wisdom, that the committee seem to have had a not unnatural shrinking from publicity. We have, therefore, to fall back on Sir William Wilde's brief account of the excavations, which may be summarized as follows:—In 1847 the Committee of Antiquities of the Royal Irish Academy obtained permission from the trustees of the Netterville Charity, the present proprietors of the Dowth estate, to explore the mound. Funds were procured, chiefly by subscription, and the Board of Works supplied the tools and plant for the excavations. The direction of the work was committed to Mr. Frith, one of the County Dublin surveyors. Opinions were divided as to whether a perpendicular shaft should be sunk from the top, or a horizontal tunnel driven from one of the sides to the centre. The loose material of which the mound is composed presented objections to both of these plans; and it was finally decided to follow up the passage already open on the west side. Following this passage eastward, the cruciform chamber and minor chambers, shown on Plan (fig. 26), were reached. When the chamber was opened, "only a portion" of the stone basin at present in the centre "was discovered in that locality; but all the fragments, nine in number, have since been recovered in the chambers and passages around, and now complete the entire." The cutting was continued to the centre of the mound, which explains the present crater-like hollow which disfigures the tumulus.

No central chamber was discovered in the mound, although the centre was reached; but Wilde adds: "It is possible, however, that there may be instead a number of minor crypts existing in the circumference of this great hill." This conjecture has been partly confirmed by the discovery of two communicating chambers a little to the south of the main chamber (see Plan).

The following passage, which I extract in full, I regret to say is the only record which appears to exist of the objects found during the excavations: —

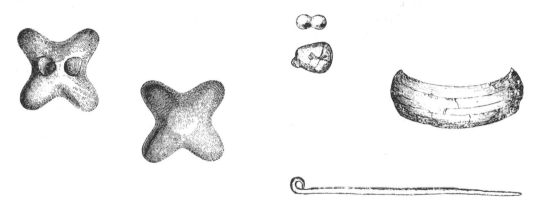

Fig 27 Stone button, jet, glass, amber and bronze objects found during the excavation in 1847

"During the excavations some very interesting relics and antiquities were discovered. Among the stones which form the great heap, or cairn, were found a number of globular stone shot, about the size of grape-shot, probably sling-stones, and also fragments of human heads; within the chamber, mixed with the clay and dust which had accumulated, were found a quantity of bones, consisting of heaps, as well as scattered fragments, of burnt bones, many of which proved to be human; also several unburnt bones of horses, pigs, deer, and birds, with portions of the heads of the short-horned variety of the ox, similar to those found at Dunshaughlin, and the head of a fox. Glass and amber beads, of unique shapes, portions of jet bracelets, a curious stone button or fibula, bone bodkins, copper pins, and iron knives and rings, the two latter similar to those found at Dunshaughlin, were also picked up. Some years ago a gentleman, who then resided in the neighbourhood, cleared out a porition of the passage, and found a few iron antiquities, some bones of mammals, and a small stone urn, which he lately presented to the Academy."

In 1885, some further excavations were made under the direction of the late Sir Thomas Deane. To the south of the chamber already open, a circular chamber and inner chamber opening from it were discovered. The former was found in a roof-less condition, and has since been roofed in with concrete. It is entered by a short passage, the roofing-flags of which remain; the roofing-flags of the inner chamber are also in position. Further indications of subterranean passages led to additional discoveries, the particulars of which I quote in full:—

"Commencing at the northern side of the known entrance to the central chamber, an opening was made which led to a passage which terminated at either end by circular cells carefully roofed with corbelling stones. In this passage were found a quantity of bones, mostly of horses and lower animals, but none human. The passage had an incline to the south. On emerging from it at the point where it met the entrance to the originally known chamber, a flight of steps was discovered. I have no doubt that these chambers were approached only by this passage, and that the entrance used for many years was made for investigation of the contents of the central portion. In the circular cell of the southern end of the curved passage were found these articles—a bronze pin, a buckle, and an iron dagger." (See Plan, fig. 26.)

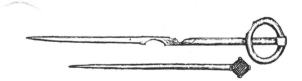

Fig 28 Pins found in 1885 *(½)*

Sir Thomas Deane was of opinion that the central chamber was originally approached through this curved passage. To this I cannot agree: the passage referred to and steps leading into the central passage appear to me to be a comparatively recent addition.

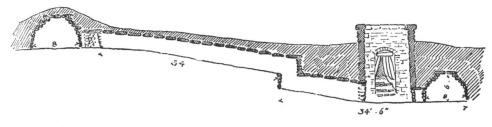

Fig 29 Section of Bee-hive cells and passage at Dowth

The cells (fig. 29) which are of the usual bee-hive form, and curved passage are built of semi-coursed dry rubble, the latter roofed with flagstones; they are, in fact, microlithic. The passage and chambers of the tumulus are, on the contrary, of megalithic or true rude-stone construction. Again. the three steps which lead up to the central passage are built of small coursed stones. If these steps, which would in any case form a remarkable feature in the tumulus, part of the original design, we should expect to find them formed of great flags, in keeping with the general construction of the tumulus. Projecting sill-stones are a conspicuous feature in the passage; and we have, indeed, in these sills a feature in the construction which would have led directly to the use of similar stones for the steps, were the latter contemporary with the tumulus.

The two bee-hive cells and connecting passage appear to be a typical example of the subterranean chambers—when associated with raths, called rath-caves—so frequently found in Ireland. Very similar chambers may be seen at Clady, some distance higher up the Boyne, the dimensions of the cells and passage of which agree closely with those at Dowth. Similar cells and passages have been noticed in the neighbourhood of Loughcrew. And a fine example has been discovered on Colonel Coddington's property at Oldtown, a short distance from Dowty. They are numerous in the neighbouring county of Louth, where I have examined over thirty between Castlebellingham and Dundalk. Such subterranean chambers in one form or another appear to have been widely adopted in some stages of civilization. The obstruction, or high step, in the passage is a typical feature. In construction and position these subterranean chambers differ from the chambered tumuli; and it will not be doubted that they are of much more recent date. They appear to have been rarely, if ever, used as places of burial. The evidence of the objects found in them rather points to their having been occupied as dwellings; and the references in Norse sagas identify them as earth-houses and places of retreat and concealment. Objects of iron are frequently found; and in several cases Ogham stones have been used in the roofing. These facts suggest a comparatively late date for these structures. The connection between the bee-hive cells at Dowth and the chamber of the tumulus admits therefore of an easy explanation.

We know that the Boyne tumuli were plundered by the Danes about the year 862. The incident is recorded in the "Annals of Ulster" under that year, and in the "Annals of the Four Masters" under the year 861. The cave of Achad-Aldai (supposed to be New Grange), of Cnodhba (Knowth), and of the grave of Boadan, over Dubadh (Dowth), together with that of the wife of Gobhaun at Drochat-atha (Drogheda), are specially mentioned as having been plundered. In the "Annals of Ulster" these "caves" (excepting that of the wife of Gobhaun, which is not mentioned) are described as having been "searched by the foreigners," and the passage continues: *quod antea non perfectum est*—"which had not been done before." It is possible that the "cave of the grave of Boadan" might apply to some of the lesser mounds, several of which are found at Dowth; and the words "which had not been done before" might imply that the particular "caves" mentioned had escaped plunder on the occasion of a previous raid. But it would seem more probable that the three caves are particularly mentioned as being the most important, and that the tumuli referred to are the three most prominent mounds now known as Knowth, New Grange, and Dowth. In any case the plundering of Dowth is fixed by the "Annals" as not later that the year 862.

The character of the construction of the bee-hive cells being later than that of the tumulus, and the purpose different, we are led to the conclusion that these cells were probably formed at some time subsequent to the breaking open of the tumulus by the Danes. The steps leading to the chamber of the tumuli would appear to have been made with a view of utilizing the latter as an extension of the system of cells, whether for the purposes of dwelling, storage, or retreat. The question then arises, can the date of such subterranean structures be brought down so late as the tenth century? Sir Samuel Ferguson was of opinion that a rath-cave, with bee-hive cells, near Seaforth, County Down, described in Dubourdieu's Statistical Survey of the County Down, 1802, but unfortunately destroyed shortly after that date, might, from the character of a Christian inscription found in the cave, be ascribed to a period probably subsequent to the ninth or tenth century. In the "Wars of the Gaedhil with the Gaill" mention is made among the exploits of Amlaf (the White) of the suffocating of Muchdaighren, son of Reachtaorat, "in a cave." And in the same work it is stated, in reference to the plundering of Leinster and Munster by Baraird and Amlaf's son about the year 866, that "they left not a cave there under ground that they did not explore," p. 25.

These references seem to point towards the occupation of such structures within the period of the Danish invasions. But I rely for positive evidence on the character of the objects found in the tumulus of Dowth. Unfortunately I have not been able, so far, to identify, in the collection of the Royal Irish Academy, all the objects described by Wilde. In the early years of the Museum the registers appear to have been carelessly kept, and the "finds" distributed according to a hard-and-fast "three-ages" classification by material—stone, bronze, and iron—so that at present much confusion exists in portions of the collection. But Wilde, who took great interest in the Dunshaughlin crannoge finds, and was present at some of the diggings, distinctly states that the iron rings and knives found in the tumulus at Dowth were similar to those found at Dunshaughlin. This would bring the date of the iron objects found at Dowth down to as late as the ninth or tenth century.

Hitherto the anomaly thus established has been accounted for by the supposition that such iron objects, knives, etc., were dropped by the Danes when the tumulus was plundered. But even raiding parties are hardly likely to have dropped articles of some value about in this fashion. They are now satisfactorily accounted for by the discovery of the bee-hive cells communicating with the tumulus, and are consistent with the adaption of the latter to the purposes for which these cells were constructed at a comparatively late date.

I have examined the objects found by Sir Thomas Deane in the southern cell. The iron object can hardly be described as a dagger. It is spike-shaped with a tang, measuring 4 inches in total length, and is more like a knife. The object described as a buckle is an ordinary ring-pin, the pin of which measures 9 inches. The other pin has an ornament of cross-hatching, or thistle-pattern, on the head. The pins are probably of the tenth century (fig. 29).

The objection may be raised that it is unlikely a tumulus would have been made use of in this way. In reply to this objection it may be stated that the proximity of rath-caves containing Ogham

Fig 30 Entrance to the tumulus at Dowth

inscriptions to killeens, or disused burial-grounds, has been well established by Brash. Many instances of churches erected near tumuli have also been noticed in the County Down, and of artificial caves in the immediate neighbourhood of ancient churches. The conditions appear therefore not to be wholly exceptional at Dowth; and it is possible that the adjoining ancient church of Dowth was in some manner associated with the rath-caves in question.

In construction the chambers of Dowth are somewhat similar to New Grange, with the exception that the roofing-flags are not corbelled, and, in general, less architectural enterprise is shown. The flags roofing the central chamber are of great size, and rest directly on the upright lining-stones of the chamber. The latter are, if anything, rather larger than those at New Grange, and in some cases measure between 10 and 11 feet in height. The plan of the principal chamber, as at New Grange, is cruciform, but smaller. It is 11 feet high, and about 9 feet in diameter. The passage measures 27 feet in length. The entrance has been recently protected by masonry, and it is not now possible to make out its original form. The accompanying illustration, taken from Wilde's "The Boyne and the Blackwater," shows its appearance as left by the Academy (fig. 30). The portion above the lintel is modern, the stones having been replaced by the workmen, but the cut, Wilde states, gives a good idea of the passage. Across the passage are placed three projecting stones (see Plan); and at the entry into the central chamber and before two of the side chambers, similar sill-stones are found. The latter are smaller than at New Grange, and do not contain slabs or basins. At the end of the right-hand chamber it is possible to pass round the stone at the right side, and then enter the additional chambers shown on the Plan. The chamber, going forward, is 8 feet 6 inches long, and is floored by a great flag 8 feet in length, in the centre of which a curious oval hollow has apparently been sunk. At the end of this chamber a smaller one, 2 feet 6 inches by about 3 feet 6 inches, is divided off from it by a high sill-stone, and closed in at the back by the roof, which slopes to the ground at this point. The two chambers, one within the other, at right angles to those described, measure about 2 feet each in depth. The furthest in is divided off by a sill-stone, and a flat slab rests on its floor.

The two chambers, with a separate entrance to the south of the principal chambers, do not require detailed description. In construction they are of the same general character. Sill-stones are found at the end of the passage leading into the circular chamber, and at the opening into the inner chamber. The first stone at the right-hand side of the passage is deserving of notice. A wide and deep groove is sunk in its face, showing nearly 2 feet above ground, and measuring about 8 inches in width and 3 in depth. It is similar to that shown in the illustration of a grooved door-post at the entrance to the passage at Killeen Cormac tumulus. Sir Samuel Ferguson describes the latter as probably connected with the mode of securing the entrance by flags dropped into the groove, and remarks that the corresponding stones at the sides are wanting. At Dowth but a single grooved stone is found, as at Killeen Cormac; and though probably its object as been rightly interpreted, it is not quite clear how it was used. The stone at Dowth is, in any case, interesting as presenting another example of such grooves.

Inscribed Stones. —Fergusson, in "Rude Stone Monuments," speaks of the carvings of the chambers at Dowth as similar to those at New Grange, "but, on the whole, more delicate and refined." This is a strange mis-statement, and probably due to hasty inspection. The inscribings at Dowth are much ruder than at New Grange, and quite devoid of artistic suggestion. They partake rather of the character of scribblings, though one or two definite forms are possibly more advanced than at New Grange. Fergusson further remarks that, "though spirals are frequent, the Dowth ornaments assumed more of free traced vegetable forms," and, "at other times," he adds, "forms are introduced which a fanciful antiquary might suppose were intended for serpents, or writing, or, at all events, as having some occult meaning." The cuts he gives in illustration of these statements are taken from rubbings, and, as will be seen by comparison with the present illustrations, do not at all accurately represent the figures on the stones. Rubbings are not, indeed, very reliable in such cases. In fig. 70, Fergusson, p.211, the midrib which lends so much of the vegetable form to the figure is really the edge of the stone, and the marking right and left is on adjoining faces, and not, as apparently represented, on a flat surface. The cuts referred to further err by omission of the various other forms carved on the same stone, and convey a false impression by being thus isolated, so to speak, from the context of the stone.

The outside circle of boundary stones at Dowth is covered in places; but as far as the stones can be examined, with one exception, they are devoid of markings. The stone mentioned as exceptional will be found at the east side of the mound. The figures inscribed on this stone are insignificant in appearance, and may be easily overlooked. A cast which was subsequently taken in 1901 disclosed some important figures of suns on the lower portion of the stone (fig. 31).

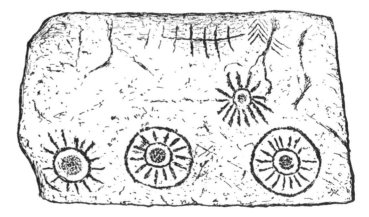

Fig 31 Boundary stone with Suns, Dowth

The inscribings or carvings at Dowth are, as stated, in general more of the character of scribblings than at New Grange. Some of the more definite forms present analogies to the Loughcrew carvings, and may possibly represent particular objects. But though possibly some few may represent familiar objects, now unrecognizable, no definite meaning appears to be hidden in them. Before proceeding with the figures already referred to, it will be convenient to notice a strongly marked example in the passage, stone No. 5.

In the markings on this stone we have an example of the same art we found at New Grange. The treatment of concentric curves is strongly marked.

The figures used in this chapter are chiefly from my drawings of the stones in my original memoir.

A few other stones are inscribed in the passage, but the markings are unimportant; one bears a sort of comb-like figure resembling some of the figures in the chamber.

The most elaborately inscribed stone in the chamber is that immediately to the right of the passage, No. 4, some of the figures on which have already been referred to in connexion with Fergusson's cuts. Two well-defined spirals are incised on its principal face; and right and left of the edge are markings which

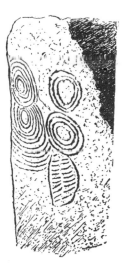

Fig 32 Dowth, Stone No 5
in passage

Fig 33 Stone No 4

Fig 34 Stone No 2

recall the fern-leaf of New Grange, but resemble more definitely the herring-bone or tree-pattern of the celts and urns. The curious comb-like figures may represent some definite object, but what we can hardly say. (Fig. 33).

The other figures on this face of the stone do not call for comment. On the edge or passage-face is a well-defined example of concentric circles. Above this figure are two smaller cuttings of concentric circles. The principal set of circles is incorrectly rendered by Fergusson as a spiral ("Rude Stone Monuments," fig. 7). Fergusson's cut is from a rubbing. A radial line is shown in the figure, after the manner of the well-known circle and gutter-markings. I doubt, however, that this mark is intentional. It is not shown in Fergusson's figure. and in cutting is not at all of the definite character of the circles; it is loose and feeble in form, and looks like an accidental mark or one made subsequent to the circles, and not really portion of the original figure. Towards the bottom of the stone is a strongly marked square-headed zigzag cutting. This has been thought to represent a serpent; and when isolated in conjunction with one of the circles, a plausible case may be made out for a serpent. But I see no reason to dissociate it from the other figures on the stone, which, taken as a whole, do not, I believe, support any such theory.

On stone No. 1, at the opposite side of the passage, a set of rather irregular concentric circles is cut about the middle of the stone. This is the only marking on this stone. Stone No. 2, which stands about 2 feet 6 inches above ground, is inscribed on the side facing the central chamber with cross-and-circle markings (fig. 34).

Stone No. 3, at the opposite side of the chamber, presents some unusual types. The flower-like figure resembles some of the figures at Loughcrew, the carvings of which, in general, present many points of likeness to those at Dowth. The neighbouring surface is described by Wilde as picked away, and an attempt made to give relief to the carving. I am not able to confirm this statement, nor are any examples of carving in relief found at Dowth, with the exception of two figures in the southern chamber. The other figures in this group consist of a cross within a double circle and wheel-like figures. An unusually deep cup-hollow forms a remarkable feature on this stone. To the left of this group, near the ground, is cut the curious rayed figure within a circle, the whole enclosed in a spiral (fig. 36). Above this figure is a small spiral of four turns. The only other examples of inscribed

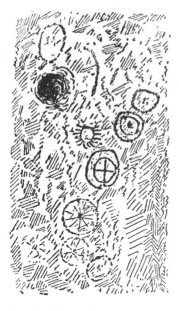

Fig 35 Part of Stone No 3

Fig 36 Part of Stone No 3

Fig 37
North side of Stone No 3

markings in the chamber occur on the north recess face of this stone (fig. 37). They do not call for special notice; the lines above and below the circle are cut in the soft skin of the stone, not picked. The inscribings at Dowth are in general cut on the weathered surface of the stones, which is rarely picked over as at New Grange. Some few cases of such picking on uninscribed stones are to be found, but it does not form a noticeable feature in the treatment of the stones.

In the circular chamber to the south of the main chamber, but one or two stones appear to be inscribed. The stones are much covered by runnings in damp weather from the concrete. Number 4 from the entrance had some good bold chevrons on it; but on a subsequent visit I could not find them: the stone appeared to be quite covered over with damp. The other stone bears a single spiral of four or five turns.

The inner chamber is more richly decorated, but also, with the exception of a few insignificant marks, on one stone only. The left jamb of the entrance has a cup and circle inscribed on it, and above this figure a rude marking of indeterminate form. The decorated stone referred to lies on the right hand of the chamber, and measures 9 feet by 4 feet 6 inches. A considerable portion of the weathered surface or skin of the stone has been picked over after the manner of the New Grange stones, and on this portion occur some characteristic spirals. On the centre portion of the

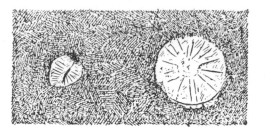

Fig 38 Unpicked markings on stone at right hand of chamber

stone is inscribed a wheel-like figure about 5 inches in diameter, and to the left of it a small leaf-like figure (fig. 38). These are cut—not punched—on two portions of the skin of the stone, the surrounding parts being picked over. It is difficult to say whether they were cut on chance patches of skin left unpicked, or were picked round subsequently. At the lower side of the wheel-figure the skin extends a little beyond the circumference, which would favour the first alternative; but the probabilities would appear to be in favour of the second. The same question arises as to the figures and scribblings on the lower portion of the stone. These are cut in the soft skin of the stone. The principal figure consist of a wheel like figure, similar to that on the central part of the stone, and two examples of a cross enclosed within a double circle, and a square figure with diagonal lines and a line through the centre (fig. 39). Similar figures have been noticed in the principal chamber of the tumulus.

Fig 39 Wheel and other markings

In the autumn of 1896 I visited Dowth, in company with a friend. In the inner chamber off the circular chamber discovered by the late Sir Thomas Deane in 1885, my attention was called to some markings on the upper surface of the lintel stone above the entrance to this chamber. On examination I was pleased to find that they included a typical example of the ship-figure so frequently found on rock-surfaces in Scandinavia.

In my memoir on the Tumuli of New Grange, Dowth, and Knowth, I have illustrated several examples of ship-figures from the Swedish rocks (Trans. R.I.A., vol. xxx, p.34). These I compared with somewhat similar figures on stones in a tumulus at Locmariaker, in Brittany, and with a figure in the chamber at New Grange. From a comparison of the forms I argued that the most probable explanation of the latter was that it was a rude representation of a ship.

The interest of the present discovery lies in the fact that we have no longer to argue from general resemblances, but have now an example which may be said to be identical with those in the Baltic.

The under-surface of the lintel-stone on which this figure occurs is just 6 feet above the floor of the chamber. The upper surface slopes back like a desk; and it is on this surface that the markings are found. The illustration shows that three or four ships have been cut on this stone. There are numerous natural markings on the stone, and the artificial cuttings are in places very indistinct. It is not possible, therefore, to make out with certainty all the figures. Fortunately the principal boat is well marked. The cutting of this figure, as also some of the others, has been done with a pick of some sort in the manner which is characteristic of most of the cuttings. The haphazard way in which the ships are placed on the stone, without order or uniformity of position, is characteristic of rock-markings in general, and in this respect does not depart from the Swedish examples. In Sweden, ship-figures of this class are ascribed to the Bronze Age.

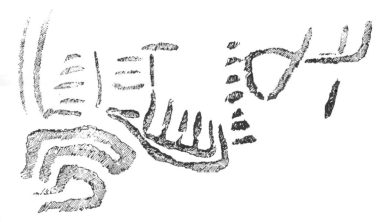

Fig 40 Ship marking

The great tumulus at Knowth, the third largest of the New Grange group, is almost equal in size to that of Dowth. It measures nearly 700 feet in circumference, or about 225 feet in diameter, and between 40 and 50 feet in height. The mound is more regular in appearance, and has suffered less from dilapidation than those at New Grange and Dowth. No trace of base-stones is at present to be seen, but possibly they are covered by the sod, which is evenly grass-grown, and makes it difficult to say exactly where the mound ends and the natural slope of the ground begins.

The mound is not open, nor is anything known as to whether it contains a chamber or not. It may possibly prove to be a blind cairn similar to the largest of the Loughcrew cairns described by Conwell. In the latter case, although the curving inwards of the boundary stones at the east side indicated a passage and chamber; and the cairn had not apparently been previously disturbed at that side, no trace of a passage or chamber was discovered on excavating the cairn. At the northern side, however, of the mound at Knowth, some large stones showing above the surface of the ground seem to indicate the entrance to the tumulus; and as a cave at Knowth is mentioned in the Annals as one of those plundered by the Danes in the ninth century, it is probable that the mound is chambered. It is to be hoped that no hasty attempt will be made to open this important tumulus and that nothing will be done in that direction without competent supervision. The flattened form of the top of the mound is very clearly marked at Knowth. A considerable depression exists in the centre portion, which gives, from within, the appearance of a rampart round the margin. A similar formation is found at New Grange. But as these mounds may have been used at various times for the purposes of defence, it is not probable that these features are part of the original design.

Some yards to the north of the tumulus at Knowth, several large stones, forming a more or less defined ellipse of about 70 by 30 feet, possibly mark the site of another sepulchral monument.

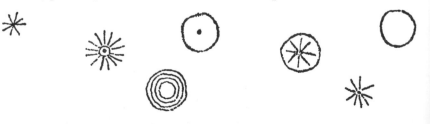

Stars and discs from Loughrew, Dowth and New Grange

COMPARISONS

Fig 41 The so-called Treasury of Atreus at Mycenae

The resemblance of New Grange to the great domed tumulus at Mycenae, generally known as the Treasury of Atreus, had often been noticed (fig. 41). The spiral and lozenge ornament on the pillars of the entrance, as well as the many spirals on the numerous gold objects discovered by Schliemann in the shaft-graves at Mycenae, gave a new interest to former speculations; but the likeness was hardly thought to be more than a strange coincidence until in recent years the writings of Sir Arthur Evans, and the discoveries in Crete, have given the Mycenaean period a definite place in Archaeology.

The following passage is summarized from the British Museum Guide to the Bronze Age, which will be accepted as a convenient authority:—The Pre-Mycenaean period in the Aegean lasted until about 2000 B.C., after which it was merged in the developed Bronze Age civilization of the Mycenaean period. In the early period the extent to which the remoter parts of Europe were affected by Crete and the Aegean Islands is well illustrated by the distribution of spiral ornament. This was a common form of decoration in Egypt on scarabs of the twelfth dynasty, and appears to have first reached Crete before the end of the third millennium B.C. It spread from Crete to the islands and the mainland; and thence it followed the amber route along the Moldau and Elbe to the northern shores of Jutland, and found an early entry into Scandinavia. It is believed to have reached the British Islands quite early in the Bronze Age by this or a more southerly route by the west Mediterranean, Spain, and France. The Mycenaean culture was chiefly extended about 1500 B.C., and corresponds with the Middle and later Bronze Age of Europe. The chief area of this civilization was on the mainland of Greece and the Aegean islands from Crete to Rhodes. It made itself felt in Sicily and Italy, and penetrated from the head of the Adriatic to central and northern Europe. The intercourse of the Mycenaeans

with Egypt, in the eighteenth and nineteenth dynasties, was very close, and is now well recognized. (British Museum Guide to the Bronze Age, pp. 117 and 123).

Fig 42 Cypriot pottery

Fig 43 Pot from Carpathos

Fig 44
Pottery fragment from Myce[n]

Without going into the question of Pre-Mycenaean dates, the examples of Aegean pottery (figs. 42-48) show many of the patterns general in the area which were merged in the designs of the Mycenaean period. The spiral, as we know, entered the Aegean in Pre-Mycenaean times, and its influence extended as far as Butmir in Bosnia and southern Russia. Into the question of this extension we do not propose to enter. In Mycenae itself it was most prominent and was reinforced from Egypt in the Mycenaean period.

With the spiral patterns, concentric half-circles are prominent, and halved and quartered lozenges are notable as well as many other designs. These were commonly used on hastily made and cheap incised pottery, the same device being frequently repeated and often amplified in numbers, and thus given a vogue which is difficult to explain as depending on any theory of symbolism; the whole series of patterns may have been used in a semi-sacred sense artistically, the same forms being often repeated, some forms being more common in certain localities. In the hands of artists and on more costly work these designs took a definite style, which reached its climax in Crete with its many beautiful vases. (See Evans's Reports, British School at Athens; Evans's Prehistoric Tombs of Knossos; and "Gournia, Vasliki, and other Prehistoric Sites in Crete," by Harriet Boyd Hawes.) The spiral is commonly found associated with the lozenge, as we see in figs. 42-48; and the spirals show a tendency to become degraded to concentric circles. These forms were well spread over prehistoric Europe.

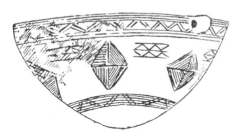

Fig 45 Pot from Cyprus

Fig 46 Pot from Calymna

The lozenge was especially used in Cyprus, being probably influenced by textile patterns, and was much in vogue on painted vases. The tendency of spirals to degrade and be replaced by concentric circles may be noted wherever spiral patterns were in use, especially in the hands of less skilful artists with whom concentric circles became a customary ornament. In Egypt artistic skill and decorative training rejected the lower and sustained the use of the higher form of ornament; but after the Hyksos invasions concentric circles were frequent on scarabs; in Europe a less developed style of decoration and technical skill did not restrain the tendency to simplification; and the more complex form of the spiral was widely conventionalized to concentric circles. In illustration of the tendency of spirals to degrade to concentric circles, examples may be cited even from Egypt.

Fig 47 Fragments from Mycenae

In the first instance, running spirals are simplified to concentric circles joined by tangents; then the tangents are broken and the concentric circles let loose, portions of the tangents still adhering to them; finally, the tangents drop off, and the ornament is reduced to simple concentric circles (fig. 49).

The tendency of the spiral to degrade to, and be replaced by, concentric circles is one of the most decisively marked features of Bronze Age ornament in Europe. It would seem that, with the extension of spiral patterns to every-day objects, the original decorative impulse was degraded and exhausted.

Fig 48 Fragment from Tiryns

A Larnax from Crete illustrates admirably the process of degradation of the spiral ornament. On the upper portion, inability to cope with the complexity of interlocking spirals, or cheapness of production, has led the decorator to substitute, for the systematic treatment of returning spirals of the original models, a number of irregularly placed single spirals. A crude attempt is made to obtain the effect of continuous returning spirals by joining these single spirals by the loose end, one to another. On the lower portion the middle row is formed of spirals joined by tangents. At both ends of the row, tag lines are added to suggest the idea of a continuous line. The lower row, except the first, which is spiral, consists wholly of concentric circles joined by tangents.

Fig 49 False Spirals
'Grammar of the Lotus'

Fig 50 Larnax from Crete

Numerous examples of the tangent stage of concentric-circle ornament are found in the Aegean and Archaic Greek periods.

The accompanying cut of a gold plate from Grave III. Mycenae, is a good example of the difficulty of treating spiral ornament, and the tendency of that motive to break down into circles. The general impression produced is that of spirals. If the inner of the terminal bands of the uppermost group is followed, it will be found to be true spiral to the centre, where it ends in a ring. In the next group to the right, the spiral gets in about halfway, and then breaks down to concentric rings. In the next group in order, working out from the centre, the spiral lives for a few turns and then runs into circles. The remaining groups appear to consist

Fig 51 Mycenae,
Grave III (½)

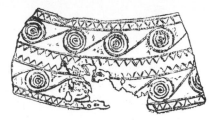

Fig 52 Bronze fragment. Athens

wholly of circles. An effect of spirals is given, nevertheless, by the outer **S** bands, which join tangentially the groups of circles in

The annexed cut of a fragment of early Greek bronze from the Aeropolis, Athens, further illustrates the substitution of circles for spirals.

West of Greece the spiral rapidly drops out of Bronze Age ornament. In Gaul and Spain even the single spiral is hardly found. Concentric circles, half-circles, lozenge and saltire patterns are, however, fully represented in Western Europe.

Spirals on the stele from shaft grave V at Mycenae

Fig 53 Spirals on a palstave

But see M. Dechelette's note, "Manuel d'Archeologie," tome ii, p. 198, where he admits that the Egyptian origin of the spiral seems contestable, and refers to the views of Dr. Edward Meyer and others.

The early spirals in Egypt on pottery are all single spirals and the outer circle of each spiral is not left free, but closed in or finished off against the next circle of the same spiral. They appear to me to be copied from grass or rush-mats made in a spiral form; the sealing up of the ends makes it hard to connect them on to the later spirals. There is thus a great gap between the pre-dynastic spirals and those of the twelfth dynasty. Where did the pre-dynastic spirals disappear to? This remains to be found out; one cannot connect the spirals of Crete with them. I am inclined to wait for further discoveries before wholly dismissing Egypt as the place of origin of the spiral, and before I can admit, which this would appear to involve, a double origin for it in two districts so near to one another as Egypt and Crete.

In contrast with the failure of the spiral westward, we find that, if we take a line from the Aegean to the North, the full impulse of the spiral system is maintained to the Baltic.

The degeneration of the spiral to concentric circles in Scandinavia has also been noted, and, in a valuable paper on the "Ornamentation of the Bronze Age in the North," Professor Oscar Montelius published a series of illustrations of spiral and false-spiral ornaments.

Figure 53, showing the details from a bronze celt of the Danish palstave type, may be noticed; it is of unusual interest, as showing the survival in the North of the Egyptian spiral-motive, and the loop in the V-space of the spiral is a survival of the lotus as used in spiral ceiling patterns. (Antiquaires du Nord, 1887, p. 258).

The following is a summary of M. Dechelette's view as to the origin of the New Grange spirals ("Manuel d'Archeologie," tome i, p. 613):—

In the Aegean area the spiral is met with in the Mycenaean period; but it is also met with earlier in the pre-Mycenaean epoch. It is known in Egypt in pre-dynastic times. It appears in Bosnia and in Hungary on pottery from the famous stations of Butmir and Sengyel, that is to say from the Neolithic period. . . . The Mycenaean epoch is the Aegean Bronze Age, and it is exactly at the beginning of this period, at the commencement of the Northern Bronze Age, that the spiral is found abundantly, at once in the eastern basin of the Mediterranean, Southern Europe, and Scandinavia. This synchronosm is significant. . . .Such an agreement, at once chronological and stylistic, cannot be owing to chance; and since, then, if it is established that the conjoined spirals of the Mediterranean are related to the conjoined spirals of the Bronze Age, how can one avoid connecting to the pre-Mycenaean spirals those of Gavr'inis and New Grange, which appear at the end of the Neolithic Period and beginning of the Bronze Age? The first influence from the Mediterranean, having penetrated into the North of Europe by the sea route of the Atlantic, touched the Armorican peninsula and the British Islands before reaching Scandinavia, connected later to the South of Europe by a land route going from Jutland to the Danube by the Elbe and Moldau.

Sir Arthur Evans and the author of the British Museum Guide to the Bronze Age incline to the view that the spiral travelled by the Atlantic, Spain, and France to England and Ireland. The whole question however, cannot be assumed to be so simple as that. It is

New Grange - the triple spiral

an English prejudice to regard all continental influence as coming to Ireland through France and England. I am inclined to think that the Mycenaean influence came to Ireland by Scandinavia, having first reached the Baltic. It would, moreover, only make a difference in date of about five hundred years; and in these countries, Britain and Ireland, the weight of all the spiral forms leans to the North, which must be taken into account. I do not desire to insist on this point, but will leave it open for the present, and wait for the more certain knowledge which will probably come in time. I may have occasion to return to this question when dealing with some forms at New Grange.

Amber was early sought in the south, where it was much valued. Possibly the spiral was brought into Scandinavia by the amber-seekers as early as 1600 B.C. The Scandinavians had many ships and were skilful navigators, as is shown by the evidence of the rock-sculptures. Whether the gold of Ireland reached them so early as this we cannot say; but Irish gold collars (*lunulae*) reached them fairly early (Montelius, "Die Chronologie," pp. 78, 79).

SPIRALS AT NEW GRANGE

To show at once the extensive use of spirals at New Grange, it is only necessary to refer to the figures; the general Bronze Age character of the ornament is apparent. The association of the triangle with the lozenge is interesting. The tendency of these forms to replace one another is well known on vases from Cyprus, and later in Hungary and Lower Austria. On vases the division of the lozenge into half, or even into quarters, can be occasionally seen (figs. 42 and 45).

Numerous examples of returning and single spirals are found at New Grange. The joining of two double spirals S-wise was understood, but the difficulties presented by the bringing in of a third spiral, so as to interlock spirally with the first two, were not overcome. Where three returning spirals are connected in one figure, we find that two of them are truly joined, the lines passing without break from one centre to the other. The third spiral, however, does not enter either of the others. On the contrary, the free ends of the third spiral are carried round the other two in concentric curves and return on themselves. Thus the free ends of the third enclose the other spirals, but do not connect spirally with them.

Lintel stone over the entrance to New Grange. *See Fig 54*

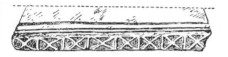

Fig 54 Drawing of the stone over the entrance, New Grange

This imperfect method of solving the problem appears to have led to the system of carrying concentric lines round associated figures, which we see employed effectively on the entrance stone at New Grange. It may be suggested that it was evolved in the effort to imitate the all-over effect of interlocking spirals as found in the Scandinavian and Mycenaean examples.

I have spoken of the architectural position of the decoration in certain cases. The most notable instance is that of the stone over the entrance. The ornament is cut on the projecting edge of the stone, and fitly marks its horizontal course; and in the lines cut on its upper face a remarkable approximation towards a moulding is shown of a distinctly architectural character. The saltire or gate pattern is one of the best examples of carving in relief in the Tumulus. The whole effect of the entrance, with its great carved stone at the bottom and carved course above, suggests the conception of a facade. Over the opening of the passage into the chamber we find again, an architectural use of ornament. The stone, as already described, is carved along its edge with dog-tooth, and the horizontal course thus fitly emphasized (fig. 15). In the east recess we find two additional examples of similar treatment (figs. 12 and 13). In both cases the horizontal course of the stone is decorated, and the ornament, so to speak, coursed with the stone. These instances, however rudimentary in character, taken in connexion with the remarkable enterprise shown in the roofing of the chamber, appear to me of much significance, and to indicate architectural promptings of interest. They strengthen materially the conclusions drawn from the consideration of the ornament itself, and add to the interest of our inquiry the suggestion that the monument marks not only the first development of decorative design in Ireland, but also of architecture.

On the roofing stone of the east recess occurs a figure of a lozenge surrounded by eight single circles, the whole enclosed by concentric curves (fig. 11). The greater part of a second similar figure is concealed by the overlap of the stone on its support at the back of the recess. On other parts of the stone are examples of circles enclosed by a similar scolloped border of concentric curves.

It may be noted that the circles around the lozenge in the figure are eight in number. This is almost always the number of the spirals or concentric circles disposed as an ornament round the

Fig 55
Spirals on Scandanavian
sword-hilts

central boss on the pommels of Scandinavian bronze swords. Following Montelius it will be observed that the oval form of the expanded pommels of the early types becomes modified to a lozenge in later types, and the central boss takes a corresponding lozenge form. The spirals are at the same time degraded to concentric circles (fig. 55).

We see in this series the origin of the pattern and New Grange. We have there the lozenge surrounded by eight circles. The scolloped border of curves which encloses the figure may be set down to the general use of enclosing curves which characterizes the treatment of the carvings at New Grange.

It may seem, perhaps, that too much weight is laid on the resemblance between the pattern at New Grange and the pommel ornaments of the Scandinivian swords; a simple figure such as this, it will be said, might originate anywhere. The answer is that it did *not* originate anywhere. As far as I am aware, outside Scandinavia not a single example of this particular pattern can be instanced in the Bronze Age ornament of the Continent. And its significance at New Grange is that it is not there an exceptional or disturbing element, but in place with other Scandinavian representatives. It is not to be understood that the pattern at New Grange has been necessarily copied from a sword pommel, but that in the arrangement of the spirals and lozenge on the pommels we have evidence of the currency in Scandinavia of the pattern found at New Grange.

The explanation I have given of this pattern is of especial interest as accounting for the association of the lozenge with the spiral which forms a marked feature in so many of the carvings at New Grange.

Another pattern at New Grange which likewise appears exceptional can be explained in a similar manner (fig. 23 or 58). It should be noticed that the broad grooved line which divides the stone marks a change in the ornamentation. On the left are spirals and a raised lattice pattern, and on the right the pattern to be described. Some cups appear to have been cut, or existed, previous to the carving on the left side of the stone, and disturb the pattern of the spirals on this portion. It has been suggested to me that the triangular or wedge-shaped cuttings of this stone are intended for celts, stone or bronze axe-heads. A more fruitful explanation is suggested by the series of ornaments from the lower parts of Scandinavian sword-hilts (fig. 56). The triangular sinkings between

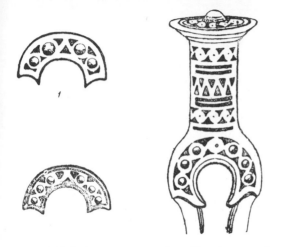

Fig 56 Spiral ornament on Scandinavian swords

the rivet-heads in these examples are derived from the triangular or V-shaped spaces left alternately above and below the line of a continuous spiral, where it passes from one spiral turn to the next. The first example in fig. 56 shows the origin of the form. In numerous examples where the spiral pattern assumes the form of a somewhat broad ribbon, these triangular sinkings are strongly marked. In the transference of the motive to the rivet-spaces, the circular rivet-heads replace as centres the spirals or concentric circles of the original pattern. Triangular sinkings become now an accepted mode of treating the rivet-spaces, and the motive is given currency as a sword-hilt ornament. The figure shows the adoption of the motive as an independent ornament.

The rivet-area on these sword-hilts is usually enclosed by a strongly marked ornamental band. If we turn now to the cartouche-like figures on the New Grange stone, we see that the spaces between the cup marks are treated in the same manner as the rivet spaces on the sword-hilts.

The double enclosing border further suggests a transference of the border treatment current on the sword-hilts, but taking a symmetrical oval form when no longer governed by the outline of the hilt. I do not mean to suggest that the cup marks on this stone represent rivet-heads, or that the cartouche figures have been copied from sword-hilts, but merely to point to the currency in Scandinavian ornament of the same treatment that we find on this stone at New Grange. This treatment is of course a common-place in developed forms of ornament; it occurs in the wall-painting at Tiryns, but as in the case of the lozenge and circle figure already discussed, the significance of the preceding relation lies in the fact that outside Scandinavia and Ireland this form of ornament is not found in Western Europe, and its presence at New Grange is now seen to be in harmony with the evidence of Scandinavian influence deduced from the spiral.

Fig 57 Boundary stone below the entrance to New Grange

The boundary-stone, *b* on plan, is also partly in relief, the ground of the halved lozenges or dog tooth on the left having been picked down, leaving the pattern in relief. On the right two large spirals joined S-wise divide two lozenges, and on the edge of the stone are some smaller carvings. of a lozenge and spiral. The illustrations will show the ornament. The arrangement of the spiral with a lozenge above and below it is most interesting, and recalls the many early Italian black vases with simple panels of two spirals formed S-wise, of which I figure two examples. The design of a spiral dividing two lozenges with other solar symbols is common on Melian vases. These examples show the currency of spiral patterns similar to those at New Grange as late as the sixth century B.C. They argue that New Grange can hardly be put back as early as M. Dechelette would advocate.

What is the meaning of the markings at New Grange?

Fig 58 Stone *a* on plan

Decorated kerb stone at New Grange. *See also Fig 58*

This question has exercised the minds of many fanciful archaeologists for a long time, but little more than absurd guesses have been the result. When, however, we consider the connexion of the markings to similar markings at Mycenae and on Aegean pottery, the question is placed on a sounder basis, and a wide general problem is opened up.

Sun-worship was the most widely spread cult in prehistoric Europe, and has left numerous traces in prehistoric markings and art. The symbols we find on the rock sculptures and bronze knives in Scandinavia, such as the vessel with a circle above or below it, representing, it is believed, the passage of the solar disc, may be instanced. The similar figure of the ship and other markings, such as the halved and quartered lozenge at New Grange, all have some reference to the sun and sky. I refrain, however, from attempting to go into this subject in a more detailed manner until the whole question has been more fully worked out.

Fig 59 Stone *b* on plan

Decorated kerb-stone at New Grange. *See also Fig 59 above.*

Fig 60 Spirals on Etruscan vases

Vases Antiques du Louvre, Pottier. Many more examples are given by Montelius in Civilisation Primitive en Italie.

The structure of Dowth, especially the sill stones and the small offshoot chamber, seems to make it nearer to the older style of such chambers of the Neolithic period, and may offer some support to M. Dechelette's view. The incised marks are, however, unsatisfactory and open many problems; that on stone No. 5 (fig. 32) seems to be early; it resembles the two eyes, probably, of a polypus, so often found with various modifications on old Mediterranean patterns which travelled about Europe in Neolithic and Bronze Age times. At Dowth no examples of the returning spiral or of joined or groups of spirals are to be found. Concentric circles are represented, but all the markings have a more scribbled appearance than those at New Grange. Further, there is no instance of the triangle or the lozenge form. New forms such as the cross in the circle and wheel forms appear; these are certainly sun-signs. Suns were discovered on the lower portion of the stone on the east side of the boundary when it was cast in 1901 (fig. 31). This portion has formerly been covered, and the suns are of much significance. The separate chambers, which lie within the stone circle of the mound, but with a separate entrance and about 50 feet south of the main entrance, show some good single spirals on the great stone which lies along the right side of the inner chamber. (See plan) The greater part of this stone is picked over, like those at New Grange, but two figures are left unpicked. The wheel and other figures are finely scored; they seem to have some reference to sun-marks. These circumstances make it doubtful to me whether all the chambers and markings were made at the same time, and we must not forget that annual festivals were held at Dowth, and that probably the chambers may have been entered at various times.

Decorated stone at New Grange

LOUGHCREW

Fig 61 King's Mountain

The spiral was probably more frequently in use in Ireland than now appears. The following will show how little interest was taken in the History and Antiquities of Ireland by educated persons down to recent times. Conwell, who excavated the Loughcrew Cairns, stated that south of the moat of Patrickstown there stood, until the year 1864, a group of twenty-one tumuli. These were being carted away at the time he wrote. Some two miles east of the Loughcrew hills, on an eminence called "King's Mountain," is a large flagstone, set on end as a rubbing stone for cattle; it measures 7½ feet by 3 feet by 6 inches. One side is incised with spirals; the other shows no trace of carving. Conwell states that up to a few years before he visited it, a tumulus stood on its site, "which the proprietor of the field caused to be carried away for top-dressing; and in the centre of the mound this stone was found, covering in a chamber of smaller flagstones, and filled with bones, all of which have disappeared, the covering stone alone excepted." Mr. Rotherham has furnished me with a photograph of this stone, which I reproduce here (fig. 61).

The Loughcrew Hills are situated about two miles east of the town of Oldcastle, at the western end of the county of Meath. From the Oldcastle end the range extends some three miles in an easterly direction. Three main summits break the sky-line, known, respectively, as Carnbawn, Sliabh-na-Caillighe, and Patrickstown Hill. They attain the heights, in the order mentioned, of 842 feet, 904 feet, and 885 feet above the sea-level. The average height of the surrounding plain is about 300 feet above the sea-level. The name Sliabh-na-Caillighe, properly attached to the highest of the hills, is frequently applied to the whole range.

The native rocks consist of Silurian grits; from these have been obtained the large slabs used in the construction of the passages and chambers of the sepulchral cairns which constitute the pre-historic cemetery of Loughcrew.

These remarkable monuments, the most important of which are grouped on the three principal summits of the range, were first described by the late Mr E. A. Conwell, in a Paper read before the Royal Irish Academy in 1864.

The cairns had been unaccountably omitted in the Ordnance Survey Maps. The omission was at this time brought under the notice of the chief of the Survey, and during the progress of the excavations the cemetery was surveyed and mapped.

On the 26th February, 1866, Conwell communicated to the Academy a detailed description of the cairns, and the results of the excavations of the previous year. At the conclusion of the Paper, Du Noyer exhibited a series of drawings of the incised markings on the passage and chamber-stones, which form so remarkable a feature of the cemetery.

Subsequently, Conwell embodied the Paper read before the Academy in a memoir entitled "The Discovery of the Tomb of Ollamh Fodhla," published by M'Glashan and Gill, Dublin, 1873. In this final description of the cemetery, Conwell sought to identify the remains on the Loughcrew Hills with the ancient cemetery of Taillten. Several conjectures of a romantic character detract from the serious aspect of the book, but the descriptions of the monuments and the results of the excavations are accurate.

A series of drawings by Du Noyer was purchased in Dublin some years ago by the late Dr. W. Frazer, who published them in the Proceedings of the Society of Antiquaries of Scotland (volume xxvii, 1892-93). The collection consists of seventy-six separate drawings of the incised stones, also some plans of the cairns.

Doubts have been expressed as to the authenticity of these drawings, on the ground that they are not signed by Du Noyer. I have satisfied myself, by comparing the memoranda and figures on these drawings with Du Noyer's writing and figures on signed drawings, that they are his drawings. One drawing is missing from Dr. Frazer's set—that of the principal incised stone in Cairn L. A drawing of this stone was published by Du Noyer, in 1865, in the Journal of the Kilkenny Archaeological Society. It is signed 'Du Noyer,' and dated 1865. This drawing is in the same style as those which were in Dr. Frazer's possession; and it would appear that it was taken from the set for the purpose of this illustration, but not replaced.

In company with some friends I spent several long working days on the hills. In the first instance, we checked Conwell's measurements, and found them to be most accurate. The compass bearings of the chambers were likewise checked, and found to be accurate, and to have been in all cases corrected for declination. An extensive series of photographs was then taken.

For general description, the reader is referred to Conwell's "Ollamh Fodhla." Borlase's "Dolmens of Ireland" also contains illustrations of the stones taken from Dr. Frazer's paper, and lent by the Society of Antiquaries of Scotland, in which all Du Noyer's drawings of the stones were reproduced. A few stones, however, which show a possible connexion with Scandinavian influence and sunmarks, had better be noticed.

It is not my intention to describe these tumuli and inscribed stones in detail, but two of the principal Cairns, L and T, may be noticed.

Cairn L.—Cairn L is 45 yards in diameter, and lies E.N.E. of Cairn D, Cairn F being between the two.

Fig 62 Cairn L

The passage itself was 12 feet long, and the entire length of the passage from its commencement to the end of the Western Chamber was 29 feet. The greatest breadth across the chamber was 13 feet 2 inches, measured from points nearly north and south, diminishing to 10 feet 4 inches where the passage terminates.

The seven chambers which composed the interior of the cairn were quadrangular and nearly square (see plan, fig. 63).

What remained of the roof was 12 feet above the level of the floor, which is the same as that of the surface of the ground.

Conwell collected numerous pieces of bones, and a number of fragments of very rude and badly fired pottery among the loose stones which filled the chamber.

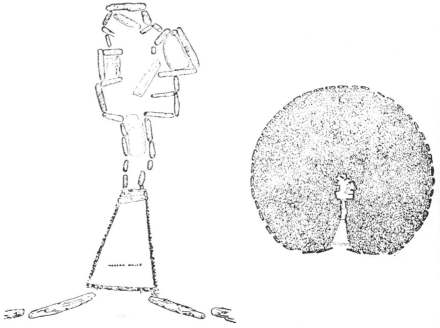

Fig 63 Cairn L. *My original plan.*

A quadrangular stone basin, hollowed out to a depth of 3¼ inches, rested on the floor of the second chamber. Numerous fragments of charred bones, and several human teeth, were found in the clay under this basin.

Another oval-shaped stone basin completely filled up the length of the opposite chamber. This basin measured 5 feet 9 inches by 3 feet 1 inch, and a piece of about 4 inches broad had been taken out of the side of the stone. It was furnished with a raised rim from 2 to 4 inches in breadth (fig. 64).

Fig 64 Stone in principal recess. Cairn L.

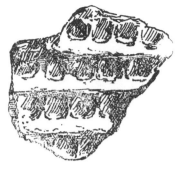

Fig 66 Fragment of pottery, Cairn S. *Full size.*

Fig 67 Fragment of pottery, Cairn L. (¼)

Fig 65 Stone pendant, Cairn S. *Full size.*

Cairn T.—Cairn T, which is known as the Tomb of Ollamh Fodhla, is the principal cairn on the hill of Sliabh-na-Callighe, and has been identified as the tomb of Ollamh Fodhla's dynasty chiefly on account of the stone chair at its base, the whole cemetery being assumed to be the cemetery of Taillten (Telltown). Although there may be some doubts as to this identification, it is certain that the cemetery of Telltown was not very far off, and it may be assumed to the included in Loughcrew. As Conwell says, in agreement with Fergusson, if this is not the site of the cemetery of Taillten, "*where is it?*" ("Tomb of Ollamh Fodhla," p. 11).

The identification of this cairn as the tomb of Ollamh Fodhla has caused some so-called serious scholars, who deride the old Irish myths and early dates, to smile. The recent discoveries in Crete have, however, opened our eyes to the truths that such early myths contain, and Minos, whose existence was formerly doubted, has been restored as a true personage.

The importance of these old myths is not whether they are true or not, but that they were believed, and races and descents founded on them, in the first centuries of the Christian period. Ollamh Fodhla, reported as the first law-giver of Ireland, died according to the Four Masters in 1277 B.C., and is stated to have been buried at Taillten.

Fig 68 Two polished stone balls probably from Cairns L and F. (½).

Text and translation by O'Donovan in Petrie's Round Towers of Ireland, p. 103.

In the Leabhar na hUidhri, p. 38, col. 2, is a poem ascribed to Dorban, a poet of West Connaught, in which the following are mentioned as being buried at Taillten:—

> The three cemeteries of Idolaters are
> The cemetery of Taillten, the select
> The ever-clean cemetery of Cruachan,
> And the cemetery of Brugh.

> The host of great Meath were buried
> In the midst of the lordly Brugh;
> The great Ultonians used to bury
> At Taillten with pomp.

> The true Ultonians, before Conchobhor,
> Were ever buried at Taillten,
> Until the death of that triumphant man,
> Through which they lost their glory.

This cairn is still fairly perfect and has a height of about twenty-one slant paces from base to summit. In diameter it is 38½ yards, and is enclosed by a curb of thirty-seven stones which vary in length from 6 to 12 feet (see plan, fig. 70). The massive carved stone known as the Hag's Chair forms part of this curb, and is set about 4 feet in from the outer edge of the cairn. It measures 10 feet in breadth, 6 feet in height, and is 2 feet thick, and has a seat-like cavity hollowed out of its centre. The front face of this stone is ornamented with concentric circles, cup-marks, and other figures; the back has been much battered away. (Fig. 71).

As will be seen on reference to the plan, the curb-stones on the east side of the cairn curve inwards for 8 or 9 yards on each side of the point where the passage to the chambers begins, the bearing of the passage being E.20° S.

The entrance was closed by two blocks of stone which filled up the passage for 5 or 6 feet in length.

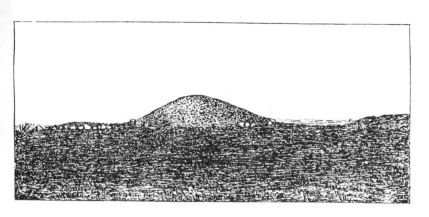

Fig 69 Cairn T

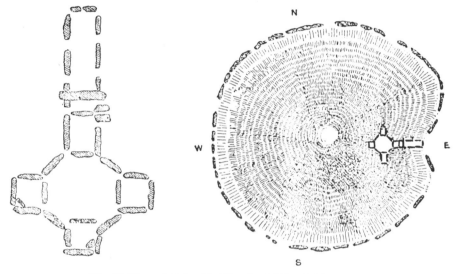

Fig 70 Plan of Cairn T. *(Tomb of Ollamh Fodhla)*

The floor of the central chamber was covered by two large flags and three smaller ones. The cairn contained twenty-eight inscribed stones.

Among the objects found generally in the cairns are fragments of bone and pieces of urns; the dates of all are uncertain, as the cemetery was in use for a long time. Some bone flakes incised with La Tene ornament were also found, chiefly in Cairn H. These latter can be dated soon after the first century B.C.

From the old legends, as far as they can be depended on, the cairns of Loughcrew were in use from about the fourteenth century B.C. to the time of Conchobar, recorded to have died in 33 B.C. Some of the pottery fragments indicate an early date (figs. 66 and 67), and many bead pendants agree with this. The incised stones do not point to a late date, but all seem to be fairly early.

Some of the cairns were evidently contemporary with the tumuli of the New Grange group. I was shown a small, clear, green dumb-bell bead which Sir Thomas Deane was said to have found when excavating the small tumulus in the next field to New Grange. It was quite similar to the bead shown in fig. 27, found at Dowth. Several of these dumb-bell beads have been found in the Loughcrew cairns: see Journal R.S.A.I., vol. xxv, p. 315. That the cemeteries were contemporary may also be inferred from the list of persons interred at Brugh and Taillten; see Leabhar na hUidhri.

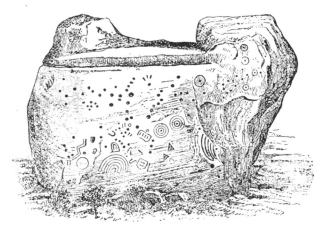

Fig 71 Assumed to be the seat of Ollamh Fodhla. *Illustration taken from the Tomb of Ollamh Fodhla.*

Out of some eighty incised stones, there are but a few marked with a returning spiral; single spirals are numerous on several stones. The centres of these spirals consist of cups or circle centres, and in one instance a rude S-conjoined figure is known. Free concentric circles, with or without cup centres, are numerous. The chevron is well represented, but only one example of dog-tooth or triangle ornament is met with. It occurs on the large stone in the chamber of Cairn "L". Several examples of the lozenge may be observed, and examples of halved and quartered lozenges may be noted in the same cairn. It should be stated that the markings at Loughcrew are all scored or punched on the surface-skin of the stones. No example, in which parts of the pattern are contrasted by picking of the surface, as at New Grange, is met with, so that the quartered lozenge has the appearance of a cross in a lozenge, but it is, no doubt, the same form met with at New Grange.

Concentric half-circles occur on several of the stones. The half-circle motive has not been imposed by want of room; it is often cut on the freefield of a stone, and is clearly intended for a distinct device, and probably represents a symbol of the sinking or rising sun (figs. 73 and 74).

Fig 73 Stone. Cairn S

Fig 74 Stone, Cairn L

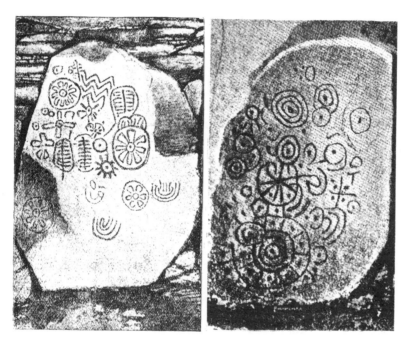

Fig 72 Stone O and stone T, Cairn T.

Some markings in the chambers of Cairn T, being covered, are well preserved. I illustrate an example from a photograph, on the left side of which can be seen an S-figure with a straight base (fig. 75). This, I conjecture, may be derived from the Scandinavian figures of birds (solar geese) and horses well known on knives. In figures of ships on these objects, the high prow is frequently finished as the head and neck of a horse, and the conventionalized bird is often confused with the horse. In this S-shaped modification of the motive, the pointed form of one end and square termination of the other are retained with remarkable persistency. It is characteristic of these curious forms, hitherto called sun-snakes. In the majority of cases the bird motive and the horse motive are inextricably mingled. The S-curve of the ship's prow is probably the ruling factor. It is difficult to say, therefore, whether the straight end is to be considered as the head or the tail, or whether

Fig 75 Stone OO, Cairn T

it is to be regarded as a bird-derivative or a ship-derivative. Such S-curves are usually associated with many motives of ships and discs. Evidence of the solar cult is abundant at Loughcrew; rayed suns and wheel-like figures are plentiful (figs. 73 and 74).

There is no reason to doubt that the cross-in circle is a sun symbol, the equilateral cross denoting the main directions in which the sun shines becoming the symbol of the luminary itself. In Egypt, under the monotheism of Akhenaten (1383–1365 B.C.), the sun as the sole god came into special prominence, until the former gods of Egypt were restored under his successor. Leaving aside the question of Egyptian influence, the sun was a frequent symbol throughout Southern and Northern Europe in all religious emblems from the Bronze Age if not from the Neolithic period. (See Dechelette, "Manuel d'Archeologie," vol. ii, chap. xiii).

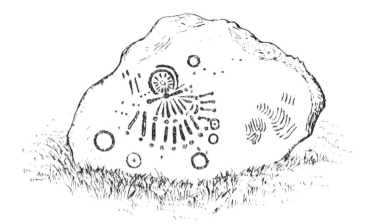

Fig 76 Patrickstown

The rayed cup-and-circle as found at Loughcrew is, no doubt, a solar symbol. The solar disc with rays proceeding downwards is a well-known Egyptian sign for the solar energy (fig. 77). On the top of the hill of Patrickstown formerly stood a conspicuous cairn; it measured 33 yards across, but has been removed. Near this is a stone about 5 feet long, 3 feet high, and 1 foot thick, with remarkable scribings, which may be compared with the Egyptian examples. Its resemblance to the idea of the Egyptian figures is very remarkable and not without significance.

Fig 77 Egyptian symbol for Solar energy

At the same time, it is difficult to escape from the impression that some scheme of association underlies the markings on some of the stones at Loughcrew, pertaining to religious myth or the life-stories of the persons who were buried there. One stone seems to be marked with a definite number of hooks or figures like horse-shoes, and this petroglyph may have some special meaning.

Fig 78 Cairn D, Carnbawn.

The largest cairn, D, appears to be undoubtedly a cenotaph. It is the principal cairn, and measures 180 feet in diameter. I take the following from my paper on "Prehistoric Cenotaphs," Proc. R.I.A., 3rd ser., vol. iv, which is now generally accepted and goes more fully into the subject.

The cairn is surrounded by a curb of great stones similar to those of the other cairns; and they are curved in towards the east side, apparently to mark an entrance to the cairn, which appeared not to have been previously disturbed at this point. The excavation of the cairn, Conwell says, disclosed no passage or chambers, and yielded nothing but portions of the skulls and bones of animals, probably ox and deer.

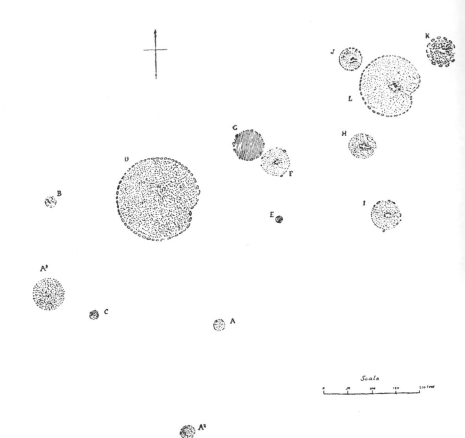

Fig 79 Cairns, Carnbawn, A - L. *My original plan.*

It may be set down as certain that no chambers were contained in the portion of the cairn that had been removed on the south and west sides prior to Conwell's excavations. The stones removed from that part of the cairn were probably used to build the neighbouring fence walls.

Not only are the large stones at the base still there, but the curve has not been disturbed; the circle of the base is still clearly and regularly marked by them. There is no indication on this curve of an entrance at the cleared side. On the other hand, an entrance is clearly marked on the boundary-stones at the east side at a point E.20, S., which corresponds with the points of entrance to the majority of the chambered cairns. Following up this apparent entrance, not only was there no trace of an interment found, but no indication of passage or chamber stones. In the other large cairns the passages and chambers are formed of large stones, and no attempt at concealment is made.

It is improbable that any interments exist in the unexplored portion of the cairn, and, if they were found, it would be necessary to look at them as secondary interments; they could in no case be regarded as the primary object for which the cairn was erected.

We have, then, the case of a cairn which to all outward appearance is a chambered cairn, with the entrance properly marked on it at the expected point, precisely similar to cairns L and T, but which proves on investigation to be devoid of passage and chamber—to be, in fact, a blind tomb. In this respect it is, I think, even more conclusive than Willie Howe in Yorkshire, as in its outward construction it would appear that a sepulchral purpose is intentionally simulated.

The idea of the cenotaph, so far from being artificial in the modern sense or advanced in civilization, is essentially primitive. It is, in fact, intimately related to the primitive theory of the soul.

Canon Greenwell who explored Willie Howe, states with regard to it the following ("Archaeologia," 1890):—

"Until I opened Willie Howe I had always disbelieved in the erection of such memorials as cenotaphs at the time when these barrows were constructed. That supposition appears, however, to be countenanced by the experience of this mound, and I am forced to admit the possibility that this very large mass of chalk stones was thrown up merely to commemorate, and not to contain, the body of some great personage".

Speaking generally, the present state of the question appears to be that cenotaphs are not yet accepted in prehistoric archaeology, though individual archaeologists support that explanation of barrows in which interments have not been made.

The hesitation of archaeologists to recognize such barrows as cenotaphs appears to be due to a misconception of the essential idea of the cenotaph.

They speak of such monuments as memorials, whereas they are, in primitive logic, true tombs.

In a most interesting paper on "Certain Burial Customs as illustrative of the Primitive Theory of the Soul," Dr. J. G. Frazer has brought together a host of facts on this subject. He has since added other instances in "The Golden Bough."

Journal, Anthropological Institute, vo. xv, p. 64.

Information as to the manner in which primitive peoples provide for the case of a missing body is scanty, apparently because it has not been looked for; but the examples given by Dr. Frazer are sufficient to enable us to understand the essential meaning of the cenotaph to the Greeks and the Romans, which has been obscured by the modern association of the idea of memorial, and render available the large body of evidence which may be gathered from classical writers.

The primitive theory of the relation of the soul, or ghost, to the body is at the bottom of the burial customs of the Greeks and the Romans. The same range of ideas which we find in primitive man is clearly present.

The importance attached by the Greeks and the Romans to burial need not be insisted on. The ghost of the unburied might not enter Hades, but must perforce wander till burial was given to the body.

Thus, in the *Iliad* Patroclus reproaches Achilles for neglecting to give him burial:—"Bury me with all speed, that I pass the gates of Hades. Far off the spirits banish me, the phantoms of men outworn, nor suffer me to mingle with them beyond the river, but vainly I wander along the wide-gated dwelling of Hades" (xxiii, 71). The description of the unburied dead and the appeal of Palinurnus to Aeneas in the *Aeneid* may also be instanced (vi, 295-415).

The notion that the ghost was a double of the body, and that injury or mutilation of the body took effect likewise on the ghost, is apparent in the description given in the *Aeneid* of Deiphobus in Hades, "with all his body mutilated" (vi, 494).

Tylor, "Primitive Culture," i. 451.

It may be compared with the belief recorded of the Indians of Brazil, "that the dead arrive in the other world wounded or hacked to pieces, in fact, just as they left this."

These examples show, however, that in Greek and Roman burial customs we are brought face to face with the same primitive conceptions concerning the relations of the ghost to the body which are found widely distributed among primitive peoples, and which, indeed, still survive among advanced peoples to an extent not generally suspected.

This wider aspect of the subject has been touched on, in order that the reader may more fully realize the force of the direct evidence of the cenotaphs.

The erection of cenotaphs is frequently mentioned by the Greek writers. Throughout Greece, when the relatives had not the body of the deceased, they erected cenotaphs which were entitled to the same respect as true tombs.

Daremberg and Saglio's "Dictionnaire des Antiquites Grecques et Romaines," "Funus," p. 1370.

That the idea of such monuments is burial, and not memorial, may be gathered from the following illustrations:—

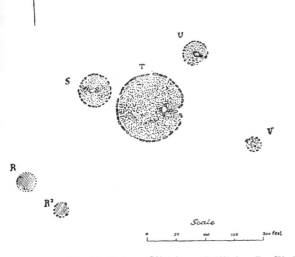

Fig 80 Cairns, Sliabh-na-Caillighe, R - W. *My original plan.*

When Athene urges Telemachus to seek for his father, she adds: "But if thou shalt hear that he is dead and gone, return then to thine own dear country and pile his mound, and over it pay burial rites, fully many as is due" (*Od.* i, 291.) Xenophon describes the burial of the dead after the battle of Calpe: he states that the Arcadians buried the dead, whose bodies they could find, "while for those they could not find, they erected a large cenotaph [with a great funeral pile] and put garlands upon it" (vi, 4. 9). Zeune rejects the idea of a funeral pile being erected in conjunction with a cenotaph; he remarks he never heard of such a case. When the sepulchral nature of the cenotaph is understood, it is seen that the intrinsic evidence supports the words.

The sepulchral character of the cenotaph, and its relation to the primitive theory of the ghost, have now been sufficiently established. In the grave goods, weapons, "food-vessels," etc., accompanying prehistoric interments, we have evidence of the existence of the same fundamental conception of the ghost as a double of the body which underlies the theory of the cenotaph; and it seems the natural conclusion that the empty barrows are cenotaphs. But fortunately I am able to relate the evidence directly to Ireland, and thus close, at least for Ireland, the evidence on the subject.

The Agallamh na Senorach, or Colloquy with the Ancients, translated in "Silva Gadelica" by Mr. Standish H. O'Grady, from the Book of Lismore, a MS. of the fifteenth century, is a topographical tract somewhat after the manner of the Dindsenchus, but cast in narrative form. It is, like the Dindsenchus, an invaluable store of ancient lore concerning glens, hills, lochs, raths, and burial-mounds. In some instances the opening of grave-mounds and taking therefrom of weapons and gold are recounted. A story on page 236 is of especial interest as direct evidence of a tradition of the erection of cenotaphs in the heroic age in Ireland.

The story relates how a King of Munster asked to whom belonged two large mounds, and was informed that they belonged to the two sons of the King of Ulidia, who were slain by the three oglaechs, and their bodies afterwards reduced to dust and ashes by the breath of a magical hound, so that "nor blood nor flesh nor bone was ever found of them".

The passage ends with the words, "Theirs, then, are the two mounds concerning which thou questionest me," ended Caeilte: "but, mould and sand excepted, whosoever should open them would not find them to contain the smallest thing."

This remarkable passage, in addition to the evidence it furnishes of the erection of cenotaphs in prehistoric times, is of interest as showing that the tradition that some mounds were "blind mounds" was handed down to a late period. At what time the practice of erecting cenotaphs ceased in Ireland we cannot say, or whether or not the people of the early Christian period had contemporary knowledge of such monuments; but the fact that the existence of cenotaphs has been preserved in tradition seems to explain a circumstance in connexion with them noted by several observers.

Mounds, which subsequently prove to be "blind," in several instances showed no signs of previous disturbance.

Dr. Naue speaks of blind mounds explored by him as "la plupart *Revue Archeologique* tres bien construits." Canon Greenwell describes Willie Howe as *(1895).* "well proportioned and symmetrically made." No sign of disturbance was noticed at the apparent entrance to Cairn D at Loughcrew, the interment in which it was therefore thought would be found intact. Can the explanation of a cairn such as Cairn D, where we find the other cairns of the cemetery have been systematically rifled, be that the fact that it did not contain anything was well known in the locality, and it was, therefore, passed over by the mound-plunderers of early times? or did the knowledge by the treasure-seekers of the practice of erecting cenotaphs enable them to detect such empty mounds without the necessity of an exhaustive search? It is probable that every series of Cairns contained a cenotaph. See Report of excavations of Cairns at Carrowkeel, Co. Sligo, Proc. R.I.A., 1911.

KNOCKMANY

Knockmany, the Hill of Baine, is situated in the demense of Cecil, the residence of Mr. F. P. Gervais, about two miles and a half north of the town of Clogher, the seat of the Bishopric of that name, in the county of Tyrone. The adjoining village of Augher, on the Clogher Valley Tramway, lies half a mile nearer Cecil, and is the most convenient place from which to visit Knockmany.

The hill forms an outlying eminence of a range of mountainous hills overlooking the river Blackwater. It is beautifully wooded to within a few feet of the top. On the summit are the remains of the rude stone grave and tumulus.

Knockmany attains an altitude of 779 feet above the sea-level. The ground at Cecil is marked 274 feet on the Ordnance Map; so that the hill rises, in round numbers, 500 feet above the plain.

From the summit the eye sweeps an almost uninterrupted horizon. At the spectator's feet is extended the ancient plain of Clossach, through which the Blackwater finds its way towards Lough Neagh.

Plate VIII Rude Stone Grave, Knockmany

Knockmany was first identified with Cnoc Baine, the burial-place of Baine, mother of Feidlimidh Reachtmhar, by the Very Rev. Canon O'Connor, Parish Priest of Newtown-Butler, county Fermanagh, in 1877.

Her death and place of burial are referred to by the Four Masters under the year 111 A.D. See my paper on Knockmany, where the identification is gone into in full (Journal R.S.A.I., vol. viii, 5th series). It may be mentioned that horse-races were held at Knockmany until comparatively recent times. The road at the foot of the hill is still known as the race road. Possibly they were a survival of ancient games at Knockmany.

The date of the tomb cannot be late enough to agree with that given in the Four Masters, the second century A.D. It may be suggested that the best explanation of the name is either that Baine was buried at Knockmany, and that the present name of the hill dates from that time and not from the erection of the original tomb, or that the name Knockmany embodies the tradition of an earlier Baine subsequently confounded with the Baine of the second century. Another explanation is that Baine is to be identified with one of the mythological Aines of the Tuatha-De-Danaan race such as Aine of Corc Aine, in Limerick, and perhaps Legananny, Lega Aine, Aine's Dell in the county of Down. This is the view adopted by Borlase in "The Dolmens of Ireland."

The second century A.D. brings us well into what is known in Britain and Ireland as the Late Celtic Period, and we have no evidence that rude stone monuments such as that at Knockmany were erected in that period. On the contrary, the interments in the Late Celtic Period point to the abandonment of such monuments. While, therefore, a considerable period of overlap may be admitted in the transition of Bronze to Iron, it is impossible to accept so late a date for the Knockmany tomb.

In August, 1896, Mr. F. P. Gervais very kindly extended the hospitality of Cecil to me for the purpose of investigating the cairn. During the space of a week I made a careful study of the monument. Under the direction of Mr. Gervais' steward, who displayed great ingenuity in the management of the necessary levers and tackle, a stone which required to be raised was placed in a suitable position for examination. It proved to be richly carved with archaic markings. The under side of another fallen stone was examined; but as it did not show indications of carving, it was not raised.

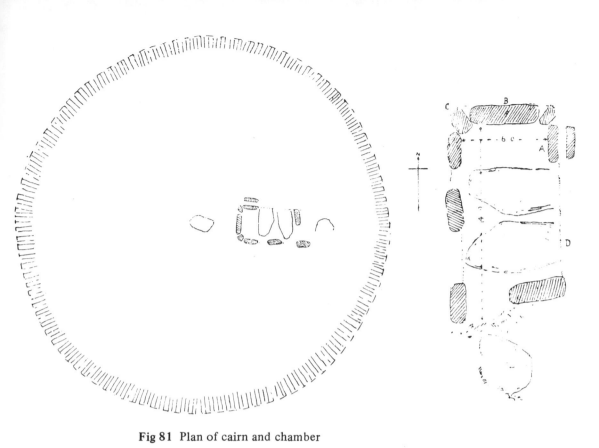

Fig 81 Plan of cairn and chamber

The accompanying plan of the cairn and chamber is from my measurements. The centre line of the chamber bears almost due north and south. The inscribed stones are lettered A, B, C, and D: stone A is split, and shows as two stones on plan: it stands about 4 feet 6 inches above ground. Stone D is 6 feet 6 inches in height, and was originally imbedded about 18 inches in the ground.

Figures 82 and 83 represent stone A. It will be observed that my drawing shows several markings not included in former illustrations.

The drawing of the stone is from rubbings and paper squeezes I took at the time.

The markings on stone C need not be figured. The straight lines across the stone are deeper and more strongly marked that in the former drawing, which otherwise leaves nothing to be desired: the surface of the stone is much weathered.

Stone B is not figured. It has no markings, with the exception of a curious deep score or groove, 18 inches long and about 1½ inches wide. It is on the centre of the face of the stone, looking into the grave, and the direction coincides approximately with the diagonal of the stone from the left upper to the right lower corner.

Fig 82 Stone A

The majority of the stones of the chamber are of mill-stone grit; the stone lately raised is a red sandstone. Mill-stone grit and red sandstone crop out at Knockmany, so that the stones may be presumed to be local. In form the chamber resembles those known as "giants' graves." It was originally covered by a large cairn, the remains of which still surround the chamber. The cairn has been dug in, or possibly stones have been drawn from it from time to time, leaving the surface irregular in places. Some small pits thus formed may have led Sir Samuel Ferguson to suppose that other chambers had existed. It is not probable that there were other chambers. The monument conforms to the general type of such structures. The chamber is not placed in the centre of the cairn, but at the margin overlooking the plain of Clossach. Though not a passage tomb, it conforms in this respect to the position of the chamber in large cairns to which access was preserved. It is worthy of note that none of the roofing stones remain. In this case they were possibly removed for building purposes, the roofing flags being more readily removed than the side stones, which are partly

Fig 83 Drawing of stone A (½)

sunk in the ground. At the same time, it is a curious fact that in the case of the majority of the smaller cairns at Loughcrew no trace of the roofing stones remains. Mr. Thomas Plunkett, M.R.I.A., recently excavated a chambered cairn of cruciform plan on Belmore Mountain, county Fermanagh, in which, with the exception of one side chamber, no roofing flags were found: the passage and remaining chambers were filled in with the stones of the cairn. In this case the cairn was intact, and did not appear to have been previously disturbed.

Some of the figures on the stones may now be described. On the upper part of stone A is a group of concentric circles with cup-hollow centres. The diameter of the outer circle is 12 to 13 inches. At the right side there is what at first sight appears to be a radial groove; it shows strongly in some lights; but as the groove does not enter the cup and does not cut the outer circle, and there is some indication of a flaw at this part of the stone, I am in doubt if it is an intentional groove of radial groove type.

At the left side of this group of circles is a well-cut zigzag of three angles. In the middle, at the left side, is a curious cutting of four triangular figures in a sort of Maltese cross arrangement. At the centre of the stone are three small cup-marks. Some lines round these give the whole the appearance of a face. I do not think, however, that it is a face. It is not a primitive face type. It is, perhaps, a modification or elaboration of the markings to the right. Below is a small meander or zigzag with rounded turns. Below this is a set of concentric circles. To the left of the latter is a strongly marked zig-zag with rounded turns. Springing from the circles, to the right, are a number of concentric curves which stand on a curious figure, with a sort of rectangular grid at the middle. Above is a remarkable fan-shaped figure. The whole resembles somewhat a helmet, with an elaborate crest. At the bottom, right side, is an imperfect spiral of two turns. This is the only spiral on the stone.

Stone D (fig. 84) shows several new forms, some of which have not been found on stones of this class before. The cup-hollows are in several instances unusually deeply cut in proportion to the diameter of the hole. They have been drilled, and, owing to the absence of weathering, show strongly on the surface of the stone. The majority of the figures do not require special reference. The most striking is the remarkable figure in the centre of the stone. Unfortunately the left-hand upper corner of the stone has flaked off, destroying portion of a large cup and ring figure, also part of the straight groove which proceeds from the central figure, so that we cannot say whether this groove connected with other figures or not. To the left is a large rude zigzag or snake-like figure. Towards the bottom of the stone is a similar but smaller figure.

Below the central figure, at the right side, is a large cutting of cup-and-rings, partly passing round the edge of the stone. To the left is a remarkable, and, as regards sepulchral stones unique figure. It consists of a double circle, in the centre of which are a number of parallel lines which meet in a chevron pattern and make a kind

Fig 84 Stone D

of cruciform figure, reminding us of those which are found on the bottom of some urns. To the left are two sets of rings, developed till they touch like a figure of 8. The lower one of these consists of unclosed rings, leaving a ridge or path to the centre.

These figures make up the principal markings of this remarkable stone. At the top left-hand side there is a letter **A**, probably scored by some plunderer in former times.

SESKILGREEN AND CLOVER HILL

Fig 85 Stone from Seskilgreen, Co. Tyrone

In a field behind Father M'Guirk's house at Seskilgreen, Co. Tyrone, is a remarkable incised stone probably removed from some neighbouring prehistoric grave, and set on end in its present position (fig. 85).

I visited it in 1899 to get a cast of it for the National Museum. The cast is now set up in Room III., R.I.A. Collection, National Museum.

On the top of the stone are some cups and rings and several stars, and to the left some large groups of cups. The most striking feature of the markings is, however, a line of over twenty cups which go regularly and evenly diagonally across the stone. A second line of similar cups goes about half way across the stone. Below these lines to the right are several cups and rings and some

good stars with cup-centres. Some of the stars have lines going
from them, giving them somewhat the appearance of flowers. The
stone measures about 4 feet 4 inches in height, 5 feet 4 inches
across, and 6 inches thick.

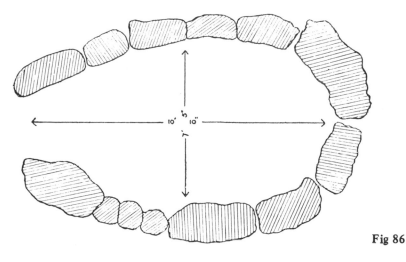

Fig 86

A short distance from it in the next field there is an early prehistoric grave; figure 86 shows the plan. I was much interested in
this grave, and wrote to Father J. Rapmund, who, I was informed,
had opened it. In a letter dated September 20th, 1899, he replied
that the Giant's Grave at Seskilgreen bore no traces externally or
internally of having been disturbed prior to his visit. He stated that
the surface of the closed grave was quite level with the floor of the
ground, and consisted of ordinary round boulder-stones, hidden
under a light covering of greensward. "A most careful examination
of the clay in the grave revealed nothing beyond a quantity of
calcined human bones lying close to the two large engraved stones
forming the head of the grave; and midway between these stones
and the entrance to the grave, a very perfect specimen of a stone
hammer." Father Rapmund kindly sent me the hammer for
inspection recently. It is a very good specimen, and like that
figured by Evans, p. 194, fig. 126, which was also found in an
interment accompanied with cremated bones. The grave is shown
in figure 87 from a drawing from a photograph which I took on
the occasion of my visit. The two incised stones which Father
Rapmund mentions are well shown: that to the left is ornamented
with some good lozenges; the other, which is the largest stone in
the grave, has three concentric circles, the outer lines of which

Fig 87 Grave at Seskilgreen, Co. Tyrone

meet together. A few of the other stones seem to have been ornamented with concentric circles, but they did not appear very important.

This grave raises some very interesting problems as to date. The stone hammer would date it to the end of the Neolithic period or beginning of the Bronze Age, with which date the markings would well agree.

Not having seen the bones, I do not care to venture further and pronounce an opinion that there was no secondary interment; but the hammer shows that at all events some distinguished person was buried in this grave. Though a date gives really the least possible information, and if it can be determined the succession of objects is much more essential, people like to have some figure; so, assuming the question is not affected by the bones, the date of the grave may come down as late as 1400 or 1300 B.C., though many authorities would place it somewhat earlier.

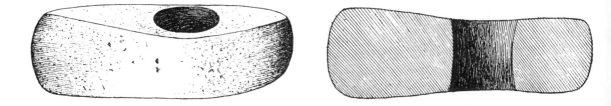

Fig 88 Stone hammer from Seskilgreen

Clover Hill

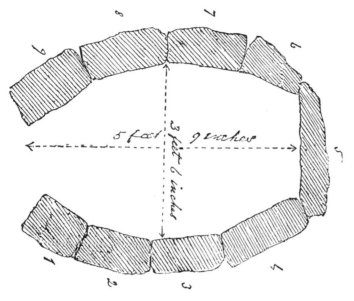

Fig 89 Plan of rude stone grave at Clover Hill, Co. Sligo

The remains of a tumulus at Clover Hill, Co. Sligo were described by Wakeman, Journal R.S.A.I.. vol, xv, p. 552, from which I take the plan, fig. 89. It was evidently similar to Seskilgreen but slightly smaller. Wakeman thought the markings on the stones of the tumulus could be regarded as forerunners of the divergent spiral. At the time Wakeman drew these stones no systematic attempt had been made to classify the Irish markings; it was, moreover, generally held by archaeologists that the inscribed spirals, such as at New Grange, were the immediate precursors of the Late Celtic spirals, and that the latter had been developed from the former. It is not, therefore, surprising, as the markings at Clover Hill depart from the simple spiral forms, that Wakeman should (although he refers the markings to the Bronze Age) have completed some of the less distinct portions in a manner that suggests Late Celtic ornament.

I visited the tomb in 1895, and made drawings and rubbings of the stones.

Wakeman's drawing of stone (No. 1, edge face) is perfectly correct, and I reproduce it (fig. 93).

A comparison of my drawings with those by Wakeman will show the points of difference. After I had completed these

From a drawing by Mr Wakeman

Figs 90 - 93 Inscribed stones from Clover Hill, Co. Sligo

drawings, I compared them with drawings of the same stones made independently by Mr. Elcock, of Belfast. My drawings agreed closely with Mr. Elcock's, so that we may take it that the incised markings shown in the figures are all that can be set down with certainty. Some of them are incomplete, but nothing is gained by attempted restorations, unless one is certain of the original form.

CONCLUSION

Fig 94 Map showing distribution of spirals in Great Britain and Ireland

In Chapter V, I have indicated the general view held by archaeologists of how the spiral came to Ireland, expressing my dissent
from the view that it came by Brittany, and then to England, and
so to Ireland. I am inclined to think rather that the Baltic was
reached first, and that the spiral afterwards came down to Ireland.
Only two stones are known in France bearing the spiral; so we
cannot look on Gavr'inis, in Brittany, as being a stepping-stone to
Ireland. The spirals there (three on two stones) are much ruder
than at New Grange. Besides, we must not forget that the sea
formed, at that period, in fine weather, the chief open way. The
land, then covered by forests, was a far greater barrier than the sea.
Crete, with its powerful navy, founded a great trade in the

Mediterranean, to Egypt and the Aegean islands. The spiral may have reached the Baltic by sea, going round Spain, or by the land-route, following the great rivers, the Moldau and the Elbe. I have mentioned how the spiral-forms in the British Islands lean towards the north; and in my paper on "The Origin of Prehistoric Ornament in Ireland," sections x, I published a map with a list of the stations. I reproduce the map (fig. 94). The late Mr. J. Romilly Allen, who took a great interest in the question, gave the same list in "Celtic Art"; and though a few more examples may have been found recently, they do not alter the description of the extent. This map is most striking, and shows that the spirals extends from Meath, Ireland, to the north and east of Scotland; but in Meath the spiral is much more elaborate, and nearer in form to the Scandinavian examples. From this I deduce the conclusion that the spiral reached the Baltic first, whether by sea or land, and then filtered down by the north of Scotland to Ireland, where it made its most permanent lodgment. An adventurous seafaring population developed early round the islands of the Baltic, and formed a rival focus to the Aegean in the early Bronze Age. This population probably, as in later times, came down upon the Scotch and Irish coasts in small parties, seeking objects by trade or raid, and thus possibly even coming into contact with adventurers from the Mediterranean.

We may now consider the classification and association of forms. Save a few rock-surfaces, examples of archaic spirals in Scotland and England are associated with sepulchral monuments, or with megalithic structures, as distinguished from rocks or boulder-stones. When we include concentric circles, and can thus extend the number of examples, this association becomes significant. Cup- and circle markings, with and without radial grooves, are numerous on rock-surfaces and erratic boulders in Scotland and England; but plain concentric circles are extremely rare. Taking this fact in connexion with the association in so many cases of the spiral with sepulchral and megalithic structures, and the association of the spiral with concentric circles, we can say that the spiral and concentric circles are to be expected on tumuli and cist-stones, but are to be regarded as exceptional on rock-surfaces and boulder stones.

The evidence in Ireland seems to tend to similar conclusions— namely, that the spiral and concentric circle are to be associated in the first instance with sepulchral monuments; that the concentric circles on the cist-stones represent the tradition of the spiral ornament or symbol; and that, some time after the introduction of the spiral and concentric circle, when the custom of combining the circle with the cup-mark, or of emphasizing the centres of circles by the cup-mark, had become general, the practice of incising these markings was extended to rock-surfaces and boulder-stones; lastly, that the cup-and-circle, with gutter or radial grooves—a type common on rocks and boulder-stones, but rare on sepulchral stones—is probably the latest of the series, though plain cup-marks may go back to a much earlier period. Cups and circles sometimes with radial grooves are plentiful on rocks in Co. Kerry, but spirals do not occur there, where we should expect them if they came by the sea route round Spain.

A difficulty will perhaps have occurred to the reader, namely, that the examples of spiral ornament instanced from Scandinavia are from bronze antiquities, whereas the Irish examples are on stone. No example of the spiral of the period with which we have been dealing has been found on a metal object in Ireland. This difficulty is, I think, more apparent than real. The gold fibulae, called by Wilde mammillary fibulae, are almost always plain. Vallancey has figured two examples, one of which is engraved with triangle, and the other with lozenge, ornaments. Save for a few fillets, in some instances, all the examples in the Academy's collection are plain. The general plainness of these objects and the sparing use of ornament in the examples referred to, render the rich decoration of an example in the possession of Trinity College, Dublin, quite surprising. It is figured by Wilde in his catalogue of the Academy's collection. In this example the surfaces of the cups are completely covered with concentric circle ornament, the inside rims of the cups are decorated with hatched triangles, and the neckings of what may be called the handle with chevron and herringbone pattern; along the back of the handle is an ornament of lozenges, not shown in Wilde's illustration. We may judge from this exceptional example how imperfect the record may be in other cases.

The ornament on two bronze daggers resembles somewhat the chequered lozenge and the saltire pattern found at New Grange. These daggers are early, and their ornamentation is rare; they show how much may have perished. Montelius classes some of these early daggers with daggers found in Italy. (Chronology of the British Bronze Age, Archaeologia, vol. lxi, p. 160.)

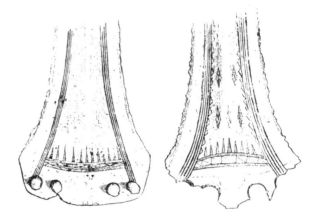

Fig 95 Bronze daggers found in Ireland

Skill in metal-working fell far short in Ireland, in the Bronze Age, of the excellence reached in Scandinavia. But whilst the engraving of a spiral on metal requires considerable technical skill, it is quite easy to incise it on stone. The spirals on the stones at New Grange and elsewhere in Ireland are not cut as with a graver, side-driven as a plough; they are punched by a number of blows struck perpendicularly on the surface of the stone. Any hard-pointed instrument, a pointed stone, will do to punch a line in the fairly soft surfaces of the stones usually selected. Standing in front of, or over, the surface of the stone to be incised, it will be found that the arm is quite free in its movements, and by repeated blows with a pointed instrument a more or less continuous line of punched marks can be easily made to follow a required form. When thus sunk, the tool may be run in the line to clear it.

Therefore we cannot, with the Trinity College fibula before us, exclude the possibility that spiral patterns in metal may yet be found in Ireland.

The absence of the spiral on metal objects seems to show that the spiral entered Ireland in an early period of the Bronze Age, before working in bronze had developed, as the stone hammer in the grave at Seskilgreen indicates, no metal weapons being found with it, though it was evidently the grave of some important person. Some of the Loughcrew cairns offer difficulties on this point, and it is uncertain whether some of the inscribed stones should be placed late in the series.

I cannot more fitly conclude than by quoting Colonel Mallery's conclusions. Summarizing the result of his studies upon American petroglyphs as distinct from other forms of picture-writing, he writes (Report of the Bureau of Ethnology, Smithsonian Institution, 1888—1889, p. 768):—"Perhaps the most important lesson learned from these studies is that no attempt should be made at symbolic interpretation, unless the symbolic nature of the particular characters under examination is known, or can be logically inferred from independent facts. To start with a theory, or even an hypothesis, that the rock-writings are all symbolic, and may be interpreted by the imagination of the observer, or by translation either from or into known symbols of similar form found in other regions, were a limitless delusion."

ACKNOWLEDGEMENTS: The publishers gratefully acknowledge the following for permission to reproduce the new photographs included in this edition: Commissioners of Public Works in Ireland, the Irish Tourist Board and the Department of Aerial Photography, University of Cambridge.

paste